THE COARSE ANGLER IN IRELA

THE COARSE ANGLER IN IRELAND

BY KEN WHELAN

FOREWORD BY JACK CHARLTON

COUNTRY HOUSE

Published by
Country House
41 Marlborough Road
Donnybrook
Dublin 4
Ireland

First published in 1989 as part of
The Angler in Ireland: Game, Coarse & Sea.

This edition published in 1991.

British Library Cataloguing in Publication Data
Whelan, Ken *1951-*
The coarse angler in Ireland.
1. Ireland. Angling
I. Title
799.1209415

ISBN 0-946172-23-4

Managing editor: Treasa Coady
Illustrator and designer: Bill Murphy
Photography: Mike Bunn
Text editors: Elaine Campion, Siobhán Parkinson
Typeset by Printset & Design Ltd, Dublin
Colour separation by Kulor Centre, Dublin
Printed in Hong Kong

CONTENTS

List of colour photographs

List of black and white photographs

ACKNOWLEDGEMENTS

To acknowledge all of those who contributed to this book would be an almost impossible task; for angling books are never really original works, they are a distillation of experiences, thoughts, conversations and views. To attribute to each friend or acquaintance their rightful credit is patently impossible. All I can do is to thank those who have contributed directly to the production of the final work and to collectively acknowledge my gratitude to the many other anglers and friends who have influenced my thinking on angling over the years.

First and foremost I must thank 'the team' who contributed generously and enthusiastically to the book and its creation: Treasa Coady, my publisher; Bill Murphy, illustrator and designer; Mike Bunn, photographer; Elaine Campion and Siobhán Parkinson, copy editors; and to Phil Browne who did such an excellent job in typing and formatting the original text.

To the many people who provided original technical material for inclusion in the book, and to all of those who took so much trouble in facilitating photographic sessions, particularly those whose patience was sorely tried by the vagaries of the weather and the photographer's craft. The manuscript was read and objectively criticised by a range of specialists, whose incisive comments have greatly improved the technical precision of the text; none the less, any remaining errors or omissions are my own.

I am grateful to the following for permission to use passages from their publications: The Central Fisheries Board; Bord Fáilte.

A special word of thanks must go to my parents and family, especially my father and my brother Brendan, constant angling companions for over thirty years, who have helped to make so many angling dreams come true. Their patience, interest and active support in all of my 'mad cap' schemes is rarely articulated but much appreciated.

Finally and most importantly, to my dear wife Frances, for all of the sacrifices she has made to ensure the completion of the book, particularly her patience and ingenuity in keeping the family amused while I scribbled away incessantly for almost a year; to my children David and Laura without whom the text would have been completed in half the time but whose very existence has made the whole project so worthwhile.

Ken Whelan
Newport, Co. Mayo
March 1991

FOREWORD

One of the many perks which came with my job as manager of the Irish soccer team was the opportunity to sample the range and quality of angling available in Ireland. And what splendid fishing there is — the magnificent pike and bream, the seemingly limitless shoals of prime quality roach, the dogged, powerful tench of the limestone rivers and loughs. I could go on and on. Most of all, compared to the crowded British and continental waters, the anglers are few and far between. I enjoy fishing in Ireland, and I know a lot of anglers who are only now discovering Ireland as an angling destination.

Now, at last, there is a comprehensive book on all forms of coarse angling in Ireland. This is not just a guide to Irish angling or a 'how-to-do-it' manual, it is a great read for anglers anywhere. Ken combines his passion for angling with his training as a scientist. The result is that rare combination — a scientist who can communicate the latest knowledge about fish and fishing in a fascinating and readable way. I love to learn about the behaviour and habits of my quarry and I found this aspect of the book particularly absorbing. It is in no way a dry or difficult text and the photography is great. It combines biological insights with sound advice on tackle and descriptions of methods and locations, with many amusing stories and scenes culled from a lifetime of fish chasing.

This book will be read with pleasure and profit by anglers everywhere, but those visiting Ireland from abroad will particularly benefit from it. The specialist will appreciate the detailed advice on locations, tackle and local methods while the beginner will find the author's sound common sense an invaluable guide in his early efforts. I hope the book will encourage visitors to 'have a go' and fish for species that they do not usually catch at home. Such angling opportunities abound in Ireland and are within easy reach of every major angling centre.

I can heartily recommend this book — I hope other anglers can get from it some of the benefit and pleasure it has given me.

Jack Charlton
Dalton, March 1991

INTRODUCTION

There is still a great deal of uncertainty regarding which species of freshwater fish were introduced into Ireland and which occurred naturally. A total of thirty-four species has been recorded from fresh water in Ireland. Of these, eight are predominantly marine and are only occasional visitors to fresh water. A further fourteen species are thought to have been introduced. This leaves a possible total of twelve indigenous fish species. The Irish freshwater fish fauna is therefore limited compared with that of Britain, where fifty-five species have been recorded. Britain's fauna is, in turn, poor compared with that of continental Europe, where some one hundred and thirty different fish species exist.

Since many of the non-salmonid species of freshwater fish (cyprinids, pike, perch, etc) have a low tolerance for salt water, it follows that post-glacial colonisation must have taken place through river systems flowing over land-bridges. The land-bridge linking southern Britain with mainland Europe is known to geologists as Doggerland. Before this area was submerged by rising seas, the Thames was a tributary of the Rhine which flowed across Doggerland into the restricted North Sea. Many coarse fish species invaded Britain through this route before the land-bridge disappeared — about 9000 years ago. As the great ice sheets melted, the sea levels began to rise and the land-bridge between Ireland and Scotland was flooded and quickly disappeared. The newly formed rivers were slowly colonised by anadromous salmonids such as the char, trout and salmon. The barren, gravel-laden rivers probably attracted the salmonids as ideal spawning areas which also provided a safe haven for their young.

As conditions stabilised in the newly formed freshwater catchments and stable food chains developed, subgroups of these early salmonids lost their migratory instinct and established resident populations. Irish trout and char stocks are now largely represented by resident stocks, although sea trout, or even sea run brown trout, do occur in most small coastal streams and in maritime lake systems about the coast.

Coarse fish is a term normally reserved for pike and perch and the cyprinids. However, it also includes such species as the eel, minnow, stoneloach and gudgeon. Documentary evidence exists to show that at least seven species were introduced into Ireland within the last 400 years or so. The Irish (Gaelic) name for the most ubiquitous of these exotic species, the pike, is *gaill-iasc*, which literally means foreign fish or the foreigner's fish, and there is no name for pike in the old Irish language.

The first documented evidence for the importation of tench and carp was in 1634. However, monastic settlements probably imported carp from Britain and Europe long before this date. Both species require high summer temperatures to spawn, and self-sustaining populations were only established in isolated areas. However, they are highly prized by anglers. Throughout the 1950s and the 1960s the Inland Fisheries Trust carried out successful stocking of both carp and tench on carefully selected waters. The programme was highly successful and stocks of large tench, in particular, are now a feature of many midland and east coast coarse fisheries.

Roach and dace were unknown in Ireland before 1889 when they were accidently introduced into the Munster Blackwater by a British pike angler. Both this occurrence and a further introduction into the Fairywater, County Tyrone, are well authenticated. However, since 1968, populations of roach have established themselves in many large catchments throughout the country. They are now firmly established in the Erne, Shannon, Corrib, Boyne and Liffey catchments.

Cyprinid species also hybridise readily and the presence in a fishery of good stocks of rudd/bream or roach/bream hybrids may act as a key attraction to visiting coarse anglers. In contrast to most hybrid animals, cyprinid hybrids are fertile. They may average 4lb (2kg) or more at spawning time, when they are most accessible to the lake shore angler.

Using this book

If the angler is to be successful on his first visit to Ireland he must do two things: he must carefully choose the water or waters to be fished and have a comprehensive knowledge of his quarry and the most up-to-date methods used in its capture.

The main purpose of this book is to provide the angler with a comprehensive review of the species which he is likely to encounter while fishing in Ireland, to give some biological facts on the various species and to list the modern methods of capturing each species or group of fish.

I firmly believe that the more successful angler is the one who appreciates the basic behavioural biology of his quarry and can make intelligent decisions regarding the reaction of his quarry to various environmental conditions.

It is obviously not possible to include in one volume all of the specialist information which is available on any given species. The reader will, however, be referred to other articles and books containing such material, should he wish to expand his knowledge of any one species of fish.

The book is intended for those who have a basic knowledge of angling and no effort is made to give instructions on basic techniques such as casting.

Measurements are given in both their imperial and metric forms, except in the case of metres and kilometres where only the metric form is used. The metric conversions are intended only as a guide and are generally rounded to the nearest half unit.

In general there is a great deal of nonsense talked about the 'proper' tackle and the limitations of using a general set of all-purpose equipment. When one considers that the fish generally sees, at most, no more than 1 to 3ft (30–90cm) of the cast or leader, it matters little to him what type of rod, reel or indeed angler is attached to the other end of the equipment. In this book, therefore, I concentrate on the most up-to-date terminal rigs for each type of fishing, and although the ideal equipment is described, the dilettante angler is advised on how best to adapt his tackle to suit a given situation.

Although I have attempted to lighten each chapter through the inclusion of anecdotes and fishermen's stories, my book remains above all a fishing manual. The readers will notice that, throughout the text, fish are referred to as 'he' rather than 'it'. This is a standard convention in angling writing; the pronoun is used in an asexual sense to personalise the relationship between the angler and the fish. Its use is not intended, in any way, to degrade or denigrate the female of the species.

It is my earnest hope that the readers will benefit over time from this book; that their bags will increase in both weight and variety as a result, and that it will encourage them to experiment with new species and new fishing environments so that they too can gain even a fraction of the enjoyment which Irish angling has given me over the past thirty years.

Licence requirements

Anglers are advised to check with the relevant authorities regarding the up-to-date position on licences and permits before commencing fishing. A list of the principal state agencies involved is provided in Appendix 2.

NOTE: On occasions throughout this book, cross-references are made. The page numbers given refer to the original edition, that is, The Angler in Ireland: Game, Coarse & Sea **(Country House, 1989). Such references should be ignored.**

CHAPTER 1

A BRIEF HISTORY

All our major coarse fish species were imported into Ireland between the sixteenth and seventeenth centuries; in biological terms they may therefore be regarded as recent arrivals. Carp and tench may indeed have been imported by monks before the sixteenth century, but such plantings were in the main unsuccessful and the stocks eventually died out. We have definite proof of the arrival of both roach and dace in the late nineteenth century. Roach populations were confined to a handful of waters until the early 1960s, when their use as pike live bait resulted in a population explosion in the Erne system. Expanding stocks of roach are now also known to be present in the Shannon, Boyne, Liffey, Corrib, Foyle, Bann and Munster Blackwater systems. Persistent rumours abound regarding their presence in the River Barrow, although the species has not been formally identified from the catchment.

Because of the widespread availability of good trout fisheries, little interest was formerly shown by native anglers in the populations of 'rough' fish present in our rivers and lakes. In some rural areas, however, particularly in the midlands, there is a strong tradition of catching coarse fish for table use. Fresh sea fish were rarely, if ever, seen in these areas and the only fish species eaten were trout, bream, half-bream (hybrids), and pike. Rudd, tench, eels and perch were largely ignored since they were considered either difficult to prepare or unpalatable. It seems that the discerning palate, which could readily distinguish a fried half-bream from a bream, had little time for the muddy, insipid taste of a fried tench or a boiled rudd! Such coarse fish were taken on a long 10-15ft (3-4.5m) ash pole with a length of horsehair or fine twine tied directly to a notch at the tip of the pole. A large Guinness cork was used as a float and the bait invariably consisted of a bunch of worms. The barbless hook was fashioned from a fine wire, pin or nail.

Our expanding coarse fish populations remained relatively undiscovered until the early 1940s, when British servicemen on duty in Northern Ireland found that the lakes and rivers of the Erne catchment contained stocks of coarse fish beyond their wildest dreams. Many of these anglers were accustomed to catching gudgeon, small roach and bleak in murky, polluted canals and waterways. In contrast, the Erne provided hundreds of thousands of unfished acres of pure water containing coarse fish of (as it must have seemed to them) gargantuan proportions: bream averaging 4lb (2kg) or more, tench of 3-6lb (1.5-2.5kg), and pike of 20-30lb (9-13.5kg). The word was out and throughout the fifties parties of British anglers became a regular feature of the north midlands.

The development of coarse angling in Ireland

Gradually, the realisation grew that these anglers could form the basis of a tourist industry and that coarse angling was potentially a marketable product. Local development groups were formed to spearhead both the promotion and the development of the product. These appeared principally in the midlands, north midlands and in the valley of the lower Cork Blackwater. To provide a national impetus for their work and also to streamline requests for assistance, the development groups formed the National Coarse Fish Federation of Ireland. Through the newly formed NCFFI they called on the Inland Fisheries Trust (IFT), which up to that time had been principally involved in brown trout development, Bord Fáilte (the Irish Tourist Board) and the various local authorities concerned, to give whatever advice and assistance was necessary. Bord Fáilte and the local authorities provided grants and incentives for various physical works such as roads, car parks and picnic areas, and also advised on marketing strategies. Although the local development groups had initially attempted to organise their own development and fisheries management programmes, they soon learned that such work was complex and best left to the professionals. The Inland Fisheries Trust therefore concentrated on a carefully planned, systematic programme of surveying and developing chosen waters in each area. They also provided bankside facilities such as fishing stands, stiles, footbridges and signposting.

Competitive angling

As the involvement of both the IFT and Bord Fáilte in coarse fishing development expanded, the NCFFI was in a position to shift its role from one of promoting angling tourism in general to coarse angling *per se*. The organisation of fishing matches, competitions and leagues at local and national level became a major function of the NCFFI. In 1966 they applied for affiliation to the international controlling body for the competitive aspect of the sport, Confederation Internationale de la Pêche Sportive (CIPS). As a consequence, Irish teams were eligible to take part in World Championships organised by CIPS, and indeed Ireland has hosted the World Championships twice in the past twenty years: in 1968 on the Cork Blackwater at Fermoy and in 1982 on the Newry Ship Canal, County Down.

During the past ten years there has been an enormous increase in awareness amongst home anglers regarding the wealth of coarse fisheries in Ireland. Originally, some winter pike fishing or an occasional summer foray after rudd or perch with the children was the limit of the average Irish angler's involvement with coarse fish. But now there are specialist pike angling clubs, conservation legislation ensuring the protection of pike stocks and the emergence of the Irish cyprinid angler.

It is the emergence of specialist cyprinid anglers which has really revolutionised the sport of coarse angling in Ireland. Thanks to the formation of progressive and imaginative clubs, such as the Dublin Coarse Fish Club, with their young and enthusiastic membership, the whole concept of competitive match angling has become an accepted part of the Irish angling scene. Such developments were greatly assisted by the rapid spread of roach populations in both the Liffey and the Dublin Canals. These fish provided the basis for winter leagues and guaranteed year-round angling. Irish coarse anglers quickly adapted to modern methods and were soon competing on an equal footing with their British and continental counterparts. When Dublin angler Bobby Smithers captured the World Championship title in 1984, it may have surprised many of the foreign match angling specialists, but had they realised the rate of development of coarse angling in Ireland, particularly in the Dublin area, they would have considered it almost inevitable that an Irishman would eventually take the title.

Other Irish anglers such as Michael Fitzpatrick, Harold Patterson and Alan Larkin have achieved consistently high placings in international competitions over the years and as a consequence Ireland is now assured of a recognised place amongst the top coarse angling countries in the world.

The hot water effluent from hydro-power stations is irresistible to coarse fish. This is Lanesborough Power Station, Co. Longford; for many years one of the key angling centres on the River Shannon

Irish coarse fisheries are often rich, shallow and reed-fringed. The installation of purpose-built, sturdy wooden fishing stands ensures both comfort and safe access to the water.

CHAPTER 2

STOCKS & MANAGEMENT

Resident stocks

The management of coarse fish, unlike that of the salmonids, is free of preconceived notions regarding the necessity for hatcheries and stocking. Anglers are willing to accept that because of their high fecundity rates and the coarse anglers' tradition of returning all fish alive to the water, there is little need for artificial stock enhancement. Coarse fish are generally regarded as rough, hardy fish which will self-perpetuate under the most extreme circumstances. Although coarse fish are more tolerant than salmonids of low oxygen levels, they are, none the less, sensitive, wild creatures which may react dramatically to any heavy-handed interference. This is particularly true of bream, rudd, perch and pike.

Marketing strategies

The management of Irish coarse fisheries has thus mainly concentrated on surveys and the physical development of suitable waters. In addition, the provision of detailed guides and maps has greatly influenced the successful promotion of tourist angling. This work was started by Toby Sinclair, the IFT's coarse angling officer, in the sixties, and ably expanded and modernised by his successor, Hugh Gough. Bord Fáilte's marketing strategies were so successful in the UK that coarse angling had become the principal industry in many small towns and villages by the late 1960s. Following the so-called 'troubles' in Northern Ireland in the early 1970s, the numbers of British anglers plummeted, particularly those visiting the border counties of Cavan, Monaghan, Tyrone, and Fermanagh. However, by 1975 the numbers of British visitors had stabilised and throughout the following decade showed a gradual but steady increase. During the lean years of the early seventies, new markets were sought on the continent, particularly for pike anglers; a steady trade developed and German, Dutch, Belgian and French pike anglers are now an important facet of the angling tourism industry in Ireland.

Stock manipulation

Obviously the demand for all popular species could not be met solely from native resident stocks of coarse fish. For this reason the IFT carried out a systematic survey of waters suitable for stock manipulation. Adult fish were taken from waters where they were abundant and stocked into suitable lakes or rivers. Such stock manipulation was particularly successful in the case of tench, and during the period 1955–75 over a hundred waters were stocked with a seed population.

Carp were also identified as a potentially valuable coarse fish and both adults and juveniles were stocked into selected waters. The first really successful effort to breed carp in captivity took place during the warm summer of 1975. It was carried out by Paddy Fitzmaurice and Noel Hackett of the IFT, and since I had joined the organisation in May of that year, I was fortunate enough to play a small part in the exciting experiment. Carp were collected by Noel from The Lough in Cork — one of the few places containing a thriving population at that time. The adults were transported to our offices in Dublin in tanks and placed in two large ponds which were situated inside a greenhouse at the back of the offices. The ponds were approximately a metre deep and the walls had been lined with dense strands of reeds and rushes which Noel had bound together and placed in purpose-built containers — to all intents and purposes, submerged window boxes! The adult carp were injected by Paddy with a sex hormone just before they were released into the ponds. It was hoped that the glass of the greenhouse would raise the water temperatures sufficiently to stimulate spawning. The additional jab of sex hormone was an added stimulus.

Each morning the ponds were checked for evidence of eggs, but for several days nothing happened. Then, one blistering afternoon, a very excited Noel burst into the laboratory screaming that 'they were at it'. All the research staff gathered around the outside of the glasshouse to watch the performance. For an hour or more the male carp chased the female carp through the emergent weeds, splashing, pushing, nudging, cajoling, demanding — somewhere amongst all that mad, frantic activity the eggs were laid and fertilised. Paddy, who is the country's leading expert on freshwater zooplankton, infused a suitable inoculation of organisms and this was released into the pond to multiply and form the initial diet of the young carp.

In late July the young fish were transferred to an outdoor pond and there they grew at a phenomenal rate. By early October the fat, chubby little carp were averaging 2 or 3oz (60-90g). A new home was chosen for them, a small pond called Galmoylestown Lough, and one October evening I released some 400 small carp into the lake. Five years later we surveyed the pond and found fish of 6-8lb (2.5-3.5kg) weight. This small, shallow pond has since been stocked on a number of occasions and has become a popular angling venue. Unfortunately, several raids have been carried out on the fishery by anglers and adult carp have been taken, quite illegally, for stocking elsewhere. However, the fish have spawned naturally on several occasions and a range of year-classes are present in the lake.

It was originally thought that the spread of both tench and carp may have been mainly limited by their requirement for high summer temperatures at spawning time, not often reached under Irish conditions. However, it is evident from the more recent success of both tench and carp stockings that populations will improve, despite intermittent spawnings, if really suitable waters are initially chosen.

Stocking problems

Over the years there has been constant criticism of the fisheries authorities for the apparent dichotomy which exists between the removal of pike and perch from trout lakes and efforts to conserve stocks of these very same species in waters being developed as coarse fisheries. The critics would maintain that the fish removed from trout waters should be used to stock coarse fisheries. However, the cost and logistics of such operations are prohibitive; let me explain.

Pike are generally removed from lake fisheries by means of either gill nets or long lines. The fish are often irreparably damaged internally when recovered and would die soon after transportation — even if they managed to survive that long. No more than fifty or sixty pike are taken on any one day and the majority are generally small fish of less than 5lb (2.5kg). The cost of providing a regular shuttle service for such damaged pike to alternative waters is obviously prohibitive.

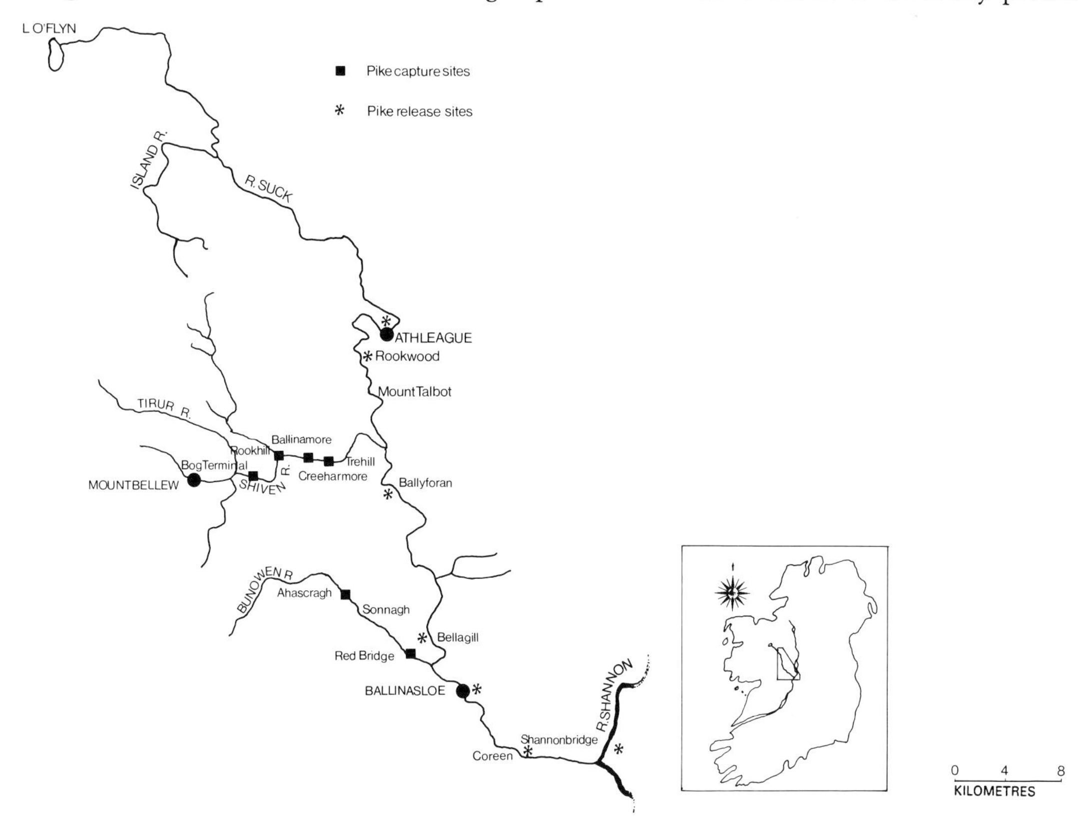

Pike tagging and recapture stations on the Rivers Suck and Shannon

River pike, however, may be in good condition when removed by electrical fishing from rivers and would seem, therefore, to have a better chance of survival. To test this hypothesis I organised the tagging of pike removed from tributaries of the River Suck, which were being developed as trout fisheries, during the mid-seventies. With the assistance of a local field crew, headed by the late Larry Burke, I transferred several hundred tagged pike to waters in the vicinity of Kilnaleck, County Cavan. Only two tags were subsequently returned to us! In latter years my good friend Joe Caffrey extended this removal and tagging programme; his work clearly demonstrates the innate homing instinct of pike.

Individually tagged pike were transferred from sites on the Rivers Shiven and Bunowen to selected stretches of the main River Suck and one site on the River Shannon, immediately upstream of Shannonbridge (County Offaly). Of the 650 fish transplanted some forty were subsequently recaptured; over 60 per cent were in the vicinity of their original site of capture.

Some fish returned home with amazing speed. One pike, planted in the River Shannon, returned to the River Bunowen in just twenty-four days; he had first to migrate downstream to find the River Suck and then move upstream for some 16km, over several weirs, to locate his native River Bunowen.

Joe also concluded that stocked pike are very much at risk from the resident fish who resent strangers being dumped into their territory. The cannibalistic pike, much like the crocodile, has one very good way of ridding himself of intruders — hence the poor tag returns from both the main Suck and the Kilnaleck lakes!

Because of their exceptional longevity, stocks of rudd and bream are also easily damaged by netting programmes. Over the years we have noted that waters under development for trout are quickly denuded of their rudd and bream stocks. Both species are easily haemorrhaged by netting (a fact which we shall return to when dealing with keepnets) and high mortalities occur when fish are released.

Importing coarse fish

It is often suggested by well-meaning anglers that Ireland's relatively poor coarse fish fauna should be improved by the importation of exotic species. The importation of grass carp into New Zealand and common carp into North America has caused serious ecological damage to both the native fish fauna and the flora. In conjunction with our own recent experiences with the roach invasion, which is currently far from completed, there is little prospect of legal importations into the country. I must strongly discourage the illegal importation of coarse fish by clubs or individuals.

CHAPTER 3

ANGLING METHODS

Coarse angling terminology

It is tempting to launch straight into a detailed description of modern fishing techniques for each of the coarse fish species. However, I have no doubt that the reader would be both mesmerised and just a little bored by the repetitive nature of the tackle descriptions.

If you eavesdrop on a serious conversation between ardent coarse anglers, you would be forgiven for imagining that you had happened upon two spies speaking in code. The conversation would doubtless cover squatts, pinkies, gozzers, tips, lift bites, ton-ups, bank sticks, hair rigs and whopper droppers. It is akin to tackling computer jargon for the first time, but coarse angling jargon is merely a form of piscatorial shorthand and once explained it is easy to follow.

I have therefore decided to deal initially with aspects of coarse angling which are common to a range of different species. The following sections will then focus on each of the major species in turn, outlining specialist procedures and techniques.

Coarse angling techniques

Since the coarse angler is principally interested in catching his quarry for sport and not for the table, there has been a general *laissez-faire* attitude towards the development of fish-catching techniques. The ingenuity shown by coarse anglers in developing new techniques over the past fifty years is truly amazing. These developments are little understood or appreciated by the game angler, whose rather supercilious attitude towards his brethren has done little to endear him to them. Their blanket dismissal of coarse angling soon disappears after their first attempt to hold a finicky shoal of bream by delicate ground baiting or when they attempt to guide a stick float through a swim swollen by recent rain. Coarse angling techniques are now so sophisticated and effective that they could denude a game fishery of its stock, both large and small, but thankfully coarse anglers are true conservationists and many refuse to kill even record fish.

Rods and reels

Float rods

Coarse fishing rods come in a range of materials from fibreglass to carbon, and to space-aged materials such as boron and kelvar. For float fishing I would suggest a 12–13ft (3.5–4m) carbon fibre rod. Try to get one with a winched reel-seat and ceramic-lined rings. Chrome rings are lighter but in my experience they will eventually wear, and the rough grooves so formed can cause havoc with light nylon line. Most float rods will tend to have a good tip action, that is, most of the bend is taken by the top section of the rod. However, rods with a fuller action, where the bend is shared more evenly down the rod, are better for use with heavy waggler rigs (see page 155).

Leger rods

Leger rods are normally 9-11ft (2.5-3.5m) in length and again I would recommend carbon fibre. You may be fishing quite small hooks at times, so choose a rod which is not too powerful. You will be able to judge by looking at the relative thickness of the walls of the hollow rod sections. Choose a rod with a good full action, especially for use with a swingtip (see page 164). When you strike you should sense the bend throughout both sections of the rod. For really long-distance work, a strong, fast, tapered rod is required.

Adapting fly and spinning rods

More than in any other form of fishing, it is the terminal tackle which is most important when coarse fishing. For that reason a stiff fly rod or a longish spinning rod can easily be adapted for catching cyprinids, pike and perch. While many coarse angling specialists might not agree, I have found that a fly rod and fixed-spool reel may be used for float fishing, while replacing the top ring of the spinning rod with a ring containing a swingtip or quivertip adaptor will ensure that the angler may effectively fish most of the leger rigs described in this chapter.

Obviously, there are limitations and the fly rod may only be used for near fishing with lighter stick-float rigs (see page 156). However, since rudd, roach and tench are all generally available at close range, the only real limitation is the size of your quarry — to land a 6lb (2.5kg) tench from a reedy swim on a 9ft (2.5m) fly rod would require more than just a little luck. A 9ft medium-action spinning rod may be used for both distance float fishing and legering. It will not be as effective as a purpose-built rod at hooking fish but will certainly provide the angler with the opportunity to sample the joys of coarse fishing for the first time. Only trial and error will teach you the limitations of your tackle.

Fixed-spool reels

For float and leger fishing your choice of reel lies between a fixed-spool or a closed-face reel. The choice is a personal one but I favour a skirted, fixed-spool reel for leger fishing and a closed-face reel for float fishing. The term 'skirted spool' refers to the rim or skirt of the line spool which fits over the body of the reel. In non-skirted-spool reels, the spool fits inside the body and line may get drawn into the workings of the reel. Choose a reel with a quick release button on the spool and, if possible, a drag system which is located at the base or back of the reel and not on the top. Select a range of spare spools, for you will need to have a variety of lines from 3-8lb (1.5-3.5kg) available to you. The depth and width of the spools is also important, so choose spools to suit the lines which you plan to use. The heavier the line the deeper the spool you will require.

Closed-face reels

Small closed-face reels are ideal for float fishing since they have shallow spools and the closed face ensures that, on windy days, loose coils of line are not blown back into the reel. When engaged after casting, there is an instant line pick-up, which is of great benefit when fishing a light float in a fast-flowing river.

Bait

Man does not live by bread alone, but bread could certainly catch almost all species of coarse fish for him. Bread is used in three forms: paste, flake and crust. Both brown and white bread may be used but white is by far the more popular.

Paste is generally made from the inner portion of a fresh loaf but soft white sliced pan is also used. The bread is dampened into a paste. Pea-sized portions are moulded around a size 12 or 14 hook, leaving the point and barb clear. Some modern anglers include additives in their paste: custard powder, jam, dyes, have all been used. The selection is almost limitless.

'Flake' is the term used to describe the flakey layer of bread lying just under the crust. Fresh flake is hard to keep on the hook and most anglers prefer day-old bread. When breaking off pieces of flake, leave plenty of rough attractive edges. It also requires a largish hook and may be fished either on the surface or on a leger.

Crust can be used in the same manner as flake, but most anglers form crust cakes by consolidating layers of dampened crust. This is done by compressing the layers between heavy blocks or boards. When dry, it can be cut into strips of the appropriate size. It is very buoyant and when fished on a leger tackle it needs to be well weighted. It is an ideal bait for large rudd and may be used even in the most weedy conditions.

Maggots

Maggots are the mainstay of the modern coarse angler; they come in a surprisingly wide range of shapes, sizes and even colours. The most commonly used maggot in Ireland is the carnivorous larva of the bluebottle, often called a 'hooker'. Its closest relative is the larva of the greenbottle

Away from it all. Two Birmingham city anglers fish for tench on a secluded midland pond

and it is commonly known as a 'pinkie'. Pinkies are smaller and more delicate than hookers and as their name implies they are a blend of light pink and off-white. The pinkish hue increases as the larva grows older. Coarse anglers also use a very tiny off-white maggot, known as a 'squatt'. These tiny maggots are an ideal ingredient for ground bait, since they do not bury themselves in the river mud like so many other species of maggot. Finally, there is the extra large soft white maggot, beloved of the fens bream anglers in the UK, and this beast is known affectionately as a 'gozzer'. At times stocks of the more specialist maggots (eg squatts or pinkies) may not be readily available in rural Ireland and the visitor is well advised to bring his own supplies.

Maggots may be dyed a range of different colours by including various dyes in their diet. Innovations in this area received quite a setback some years ago when it was discovered that the most popular of these dyes, Chrysadine, was highly carcinogenic and had led to the deaths of several well-known coarse anglers. Diluting the dye or handling stained maggots coloured their hands and the carcinogen was gradually absorbed into the blood stream. However, modern dyes are quite safe. Maggots dyed red have become increasingly popular in recent years in Ireland and are now extensively used by many of the more successful match anglers.

Before use, it is often advisable to clean the maggots by storing them in containers of maize or sawdust overnight. This ensures that the maggots are dry and scaly to the touch and have not begun to 'sweat'. Remember to leave plenty of air in your storage containers and ideally you should place these in a fridge. Many ardent coarse anglers purchase a second-hand fridge specifically for this purpose.

Maggots are at their best when the feeding spot, situated at the pointed end of the maggot, is just visible. Always hook your maggots through the blunt end as this greatly improves hooking success.

Casters

If maggots are allowed to continue their development they quickly change from larva into a reddish-brown pupa known as a 'caster'. Anglers normally make their own casters but it is also possible to buy them from bait stockists. You may generally assume that 1 gallon (4.5l) of maggots will give you 6 pints (3.5l) of casters.

Making casters is quite a tedious business. Take your container of white maggots out of the fridge and carefully watch for the appearance of the quiescent casters. As soon as some appear, pour your maggots into a sieve or riddle with apertures of 3-5mm and allow the maggots to work their way through the spaces in the riddle. The casters may need to be riddled two or three times a day. Each time you will be left with a mixture of dead maggot skins and casters.

Separate out the casters and store them in sealed plastic bags in the fridge. You may also store your casters in a suitable box; a good trick is to cover them with some wet newspaper. Place a sheet of plastic on top of this and seal with an airtight lid. Holding casters may be problematical, for your aim is to stop their development but not to kill them. If they do die, you are soon reminded of this fact, for your box will contain nothing but a soggy, wet, smelly mess of putrid liquid. But if everything goes according to plan, your casters should stay fresh for two to three days in the fridge.

If you allow development to continue, the maggots will soon become buoyant and are then known as floaters. These make excellent hook bait but are a disaster in ground bait since they disperse willy-nilly throughout the water column. On warm days a bag of carefully nurtured casters may become floaters in as little as three to four hours.

Sinking casters may be used either as bait or as ground bait. A cocktail of worm and caster can be very effective for Irish bream.

Worms

Worms are also a standard bait for coarse fish. As in the case of the salmonids, lobworms, blackheads, redworms and the yellow-striped brandlings may be used. In general I have found the redworms and brandlings to work best under Irish conditions. Of the two, the redworm is probably the most effective and easiest to handle. It is less brittle than the brandling and closely resembles the common aquatic worms known as *Oligochaetes*. Now for the nasty part — their collection. Redworms inhabit the most obnoxious places: manure heaps, compost heaps, cow pats, all have their populations of such worms. The easiest method of propagating your own colony of redworms (or brandlings) is to make a wormery in your garden. This is quite a simple procedure and basically involves collecting all of the biodegradable rubbish into a selected corner of the garden: bits of vegetables, tea leaves, grease, are all ideal components. Start your wormery off with some straw and a little fresh manure and then simply continue to pour on kitchen leftovers. Avoid grass cuttings as these are slow to decompose and may retard the development of your wormery. An initial seeding of redworms or brandlings should be sufficient to ensure a healthy colony. When going fishing the worms may be stored in a dampened mixture of 10 per cent soil and 90 per cent moss peat. If you keep the mixture damp, worms will survive for many months in such a concoction.

Seed bait

With the advent of roach into our systems, anglers are now becoming conscious of the advantages of fishing hempseed. Boiled hemp is an excellent bait or ground bait for roach, particularly during warm summer weather. It is, however, quite a tedious bait to hook mount and in recent years artificial hemp has become very popular, particularly with pole match-anglers. Seeds known as 'tares' are also growing in popularity. Seed bait is invariably used as a float bait.

Baiting the swim

Ground baiting

Ground bait is used to attract and hold feeding fish in a chosen swim. The angler attempts to create an atmosphere of competition amongst the fish and it is best to adopt the maxim of little and often. Initial ground baiting for bream is the exception to this rule, when quite appreciable quantities may be required to attract the feeding shoals. In richer, little fished waters it may take several days to wean the fish onto the baits we think they should like and an initial heavy pre-baiting may be required.

Ground bait is basically composed of pure bread — brown or white or a mixture of the two. White bread tends to bind the balls of ground bait. Into the basic ground bait mix one may add worms, casters, maggots or chopped worms. The larger maggots and whole worms tend to squirm and burrow throughout the ground bait and often cause it to disintegrate in mid-air; hence the use of squatts, casters or chopped worms.

Additives are also used in ground baiting and substances such as rice, breakfast cereals, rusk, custard powder, peanuts, have all been used. The list of potentially useful materials is almost limitless and great satisfaction may be gained from inventing a secret concoction which is particularly effective on a heavily fished water.

To mix the ground bait, fill your mixing bowl or bucket to the desired level with water. Add a mixture of white and brown bread, remembering that the greater the proportion of white crumb, the firmer the resultant ground bait. Be careful not to add too much additional material, such as maggots or chopped worms. Dampening your hands before moulding each ball of ground bait will ensure that an even, rotund sphere is formed.

Balls of ground bait are variable in size but the maximum would be the size of a cricket ball. It is more usual to mix balls the size of golf balls or slightly smaller and to disperse these using a purpose-made catapult. By far the best make is the whopper dropper. Remember that great balls of ground bait smashing at random into a relatively shallow swim will do little more than scare every fish in the vicinity. Be circumspect with your ground baiting and plan your tactics carefully. Before ground baiting, remember to plumb the depth (see page 163) and insert the ground bait several minutes before starting to fish with hook bait.

The second form of ground baiting, known as loose feeding, involves the intermittent addition of loose maggots or casters to the swim. It is normally used when fishing near the surface for rudd

Overloaded with squirming maggots, this ball of ground bait is destined to disintegrate in mid-air

1. Red and white maggots
2. Casters

Two fine bronze bream from the River Erne, near Enniskillen, Co. Fermanagh

Meticulous attention to detail and quality matching tackle are the hallmarks of the carp specialist

An ideal swim on the Royal Canal (Photo courtesy CFB)

or roach but can be useful for a whole range of species in clear, relatively shallow waters, such as the Royal and Grand Canals.

Pre-baiting a swim

Pre-baiting will not alone attract fish but it will, more importantly, wean them onto the hook bait. The chosen swim is fed with ground bait on several occasions prior to the first fishing session. Since you are attempting to entice a set feeding behaviour in the fish, keep your ground bait simple. A whole variety of substances may only serve to confuse the fish's palate and although he may fancy all of them, the angler will find it nearly impossible to gauge which bait he prefers on any given day.

Bait may also be added to your swim by means of a swim feeder. This is attached directly to your main line and it comes in a variety of shapes and sizes, but basically it is a holed plastic container into which you normally stuff a mixture of ground bait and maggots. The great advantage of the swim feeder is that it does just that — feeds your exact swim every time. The maggots crawl out through the holes and push the ground bait in front of them. If you use dry ground bait, it forms a cloud as it floats out of the feeder. In faster rivers the current can do an excellent job at washing out the bait. Modern swim feeders have caps, one of which is removed to fill the containers. In rivers you should use as little weight as possible and have the feeder just about holding station in the current. It will have the added advantage of offering less solid resistance to a biting fish.

When fishing a really rough bottom, a good trick is to use a running swivel rig, which will mean that the fish can be hooked without having to dislodge the feeder. The fish's movements after it is hooked will invariably pull the feeder free.

Floats

Floats come in a variety of forms and shapes. Whole books have been written on the art of float fishing and its related technology. The three principal types of float used in Ireland are the waggler, the stick float and my own particular favourite, the slider or sliding float. Each float is designed to cock with the addition of a given quantity of lead shot; this is clearly marked on the stem or butt of the float (ie 2 Swan, 5 BB, 2 AAA, etc).

Wagglers

Wagglers are used in slow-flowing rivers, canals and lakes. They come in a variety of different materials — cane, plastic and peacock quill — and take two basic forms — straight wagglers and body wagglers. Body wagglers are used under windy conditions. With a waggler, the line is filtered through a fine wire ring at the base of the float. A lead shot is placed fore and aft and thus the float is retained firmly between the two shot. The remaining cast below the float is carefully shotted so that the float cocks with just its tip showing above the surface. Shotting floats is an art but when bulk shotting a waggler you should aim to have some 80 per cent of the total cocking weight just below the float. Remember to place the larger shot on the cast first and then the smaller shot in decreasing order of diameter. This will help in casting the float since you should aim to ensure that the rig or cast falls in a line on the surface of the water. Different distributions of the lead shot will result in the bait dropping at different rates. For example, bulk shotting on a long tail will ensure that the hooked bait falls really slowly through the water column.

Wagglers are mainly used in stillwater conditions, whether on lakes or rivers. To hasten the speed with which floats may be changed, float adaptors are now often used. Various sizes of waggler may be simply slotted into the adaptor and the shot loading varied to suit the new float. Tip inserts are also widely used to increase sensitivity but these are most useful under very calm conditions.

When float fishing for coarse fish, a bite will be indicated either by the float disappearing under water or by the stem of the float rising higher in the water — the so-called lift bite. To trigger this bite the float is often rigged with a single BB acting as the trigger. Also remember to test how far you can comfortably cast the float you intend to use before feeding the swim.

Stick floats

Stick floats are normally a balanced mixture of cane and balsa wood but wire-stemmed varieties are also popular. They are principally used in flowing water and offer a far better presentation than the waggler. There are two classic shotting patterns: the bulk shotting method and the stringer or shirt-button method. The line is held in place at the top and bottom of the float by means of a small purpose-made elastic band. The stick float rig is cast sideways out into the stream and allowed to move down with the current. To avoid drag the line is mended, but in really fast water it may be necessary to hold against the float, and in such situations some over-shotting may be necessary; this ensures that the presentation is not ruined by the float's tendency to rise with the increased pressure.

Slider floats

When waggler fishing, the angler cannot effectively fish depths greater than the length of his rod. Slider floats were designed to overcome such problems. The slider is a waggler which is free to move along the main line. As the shot sinks, the line is pulled through the base ring until the preset stop is reached. The stop itself is so designed that it will slip cleanly through the rod rings.

Pole fishing is particularly popular along the Dublin canals. Irish international Alan Larkin, fishing the Royal Canal at Castleknock, Dublin

Old red eye. A good 4lb tench for Mike Bunn from Fin Lough, Co. Sligo

Pike plugs are most effective during the warmer months of the year

One of the most handsome of our freshwater fish — the perch

A selection of the author's favourite pike baits, old and modern

12
14
16
18
20
22
PATENT
No3

It generally comprises a piece of nylon tied onto the main line by means of a specific knot. It is an excellent way to plumb depth and can be used with surprising sensitivity even at 5 to 6m. Some anglers insert a smaller shot on the line to prevent the float slipping down onto the bulk shot and running the risk of the base ring sticking onto one of the shot; it also helps to prevent tangles. The new rubber leger stops are also ideal for use with a slider. Do not confine your slider float fishing to times when you need to fish at great depths. It can be a surprisingly versatile and effective method. The key to success with the slider is experimentation.

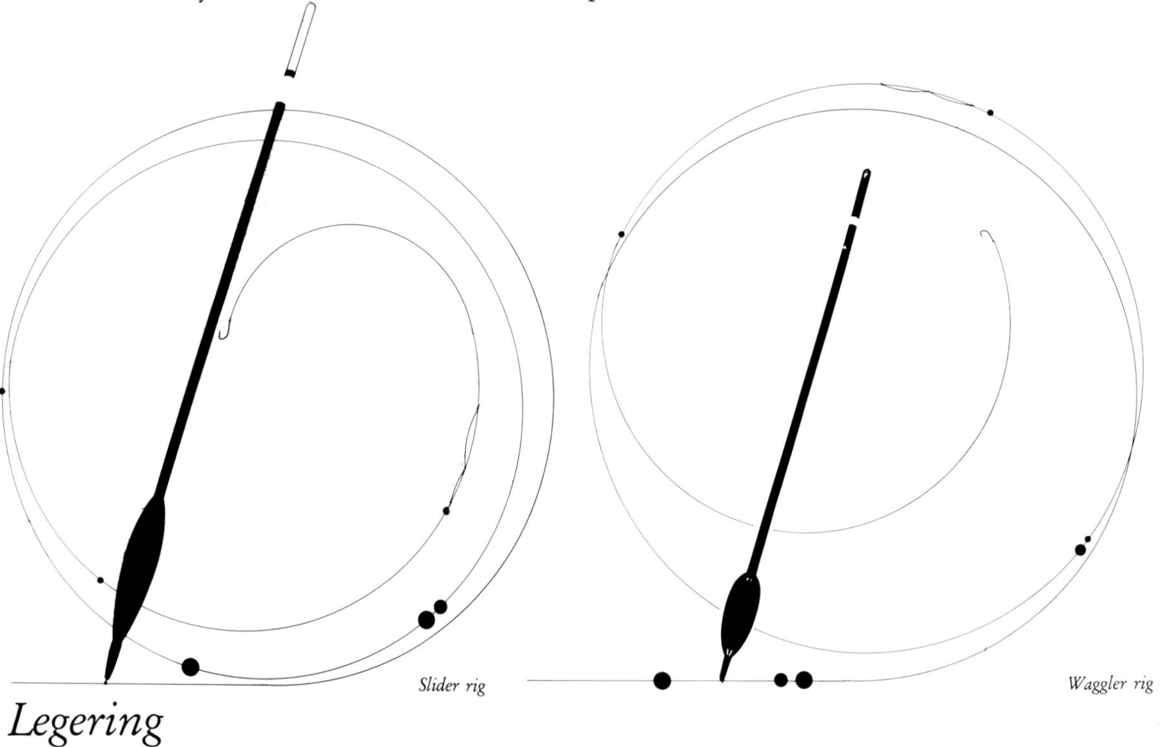
Slider rig　*Waggler rig*

Legering

Legering, despite impressions often held to the contrary, is an extremely sensitive and versatile method of fishing. It may be used in practically every situation except in the most heavily weeded swims and it has the advantage of being less complicated and easier to master than float fishing. The principal key to successful legering is a good method of discerning bites both quickly and unequivocally.

Swingtips

The original bite indicators were rather cumbersome affairs connected to the butt of the rod just above the rod handle. Known as butt indicators, they were super-sensitive but time-consuming and tedious to re-set. They were replaced by the swingtip, a system of bite indication which revolutionised static methods of coarse fishing. The swingtip consists of an 8 to 18in (20–45cm) addition to the rod which is connected by means of a screw fitting to a metal sleeve which is built into the top rod ring. The screw fitting is connected either to an extruded piece of plastic or rubber which slips tightly over the base of the tip. The longer the tip the more sensitive it is but the great disadvantage of the swingtip is that it needs relatively calm conditions to function properly.

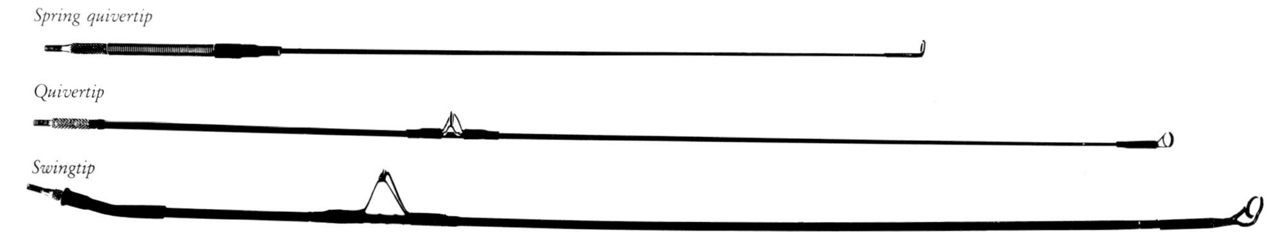

Quivertips

To overcome such problems quivertips were developed. These stiff, highly flexible additions to the top ring are ideal for use under windy conditions or in flowing water. These offer less resistance to a fish which has taken the bait and in the more modern versions the tip may be moved in and out of the mount, thus reducing tension. When fully extended, a long springtip is as sensitive as a swingtip. They are now available in a range of different strengths to suit varying wind and water conditions.

Target boards

At times even the most sensitive of tips are inadequate in sensing delicate bites. Target boards were designed to give a measure of the degree of movement of the tip. Using a target board the angler may differentiate between movements caused by the stream, which are normally cyclical and regular, and the more definite but none the less tiny bites of delicately feeding fish. Target boards are made from either clear plastic or white board and have a series of fan-shaped dark lines painted onto their surface. The tip is placed either against the board, which is mounted on a bank stick, or in the case of a swingtip may hang over the top of the notched clear plastic screen.

Rudd and roach (on right), all taken on a slider float in 3m of water

Dublin angler Derry Ryan lovingly cradles a 20lb pike taken in Muddy Lake, near Shercock, Co. Cavan

Positioning the rod

When legering, the positioning of the rod is critical. The rod rests must be so arranged that the tip is as near to the surface as possible. Some of the greatest exponents of the swingtip, such as England's Sid Meads, are so loath to change to a quivertip that even under windy conditions they will actually fish an extra long swingtip, set just under the surface. When a fish bites, the tip surfaces and the angler strikes.

The rig is cast out directly in front of the angler into an area which has previously been baited. The bomb is allowed to sink. When it has reached the bottom the tip becomes flaccid and the angler tightens into the bomb and moves the rod into the rod rests, which have been set so as to ensure a 90° angle between the tip and the line.

When a bite comes, do not be too quick to strike, but let it develop for a few moments. Then raise the rod and strike, sweeping the rod back and to the side. Never stand too close to an angler who is legering, for when a bite comes he must give a very exaggerated strike to ensure that he takes the belly out of the line and lifts the lead off the bottom.

Leger rigs

The more commonly used leger rig consists of a basic bomb, snood, tail arrangement. Bombs may vary in weight from a fraction of an ounce to 2oz (56g), but generally ½–1oz (14–28g) bombs are adequate even when fishing a relatively wide river. Because of the extra weight the main line should be at least 4lb (2kg) but a lighter tail of 2–3lb (1–1.5kg) may be used under clear water conditions. The strength of the tail is, of course, directly related to hook size; the smaller the hook the lighter the line.

Pole fishing

It is claimed that the pole is a recent invention, developed by continental anglers to enhance speed and delicate presentation. Certainly the modern, light, synthetic pole is relatively new but the basic principle must stretch well back into the ages of pre-history. The technique is simplicity itself: a long, light, carbon pole, up to 11m in length and divided into easily handled sections, is used to simply drop a bait into the desired area. No casting is required and the line is attached either directly to a ring on the tip of the pole or to a piece of supple elastic. The line may also run through the hollow pole where it is again attached to an extensible piece of elastic.

The pole allows the use of the finest of lines, hooks and floats. It is principally a match rod where speed and delicacy are the main objectives. A good pole angler will rate his performance on the number of fish handled per minute! Pole anglers have also developed the principle of layer ground baiting where specific zones of the water column may be preferentially fed. This technique has, I believe, much wider application and I will cover it in a little more detail in the section on bream (see page 182).

Hooks

Selection of hooks

The choice of hooks is very important in coarse fishing since it will greatly influence the presentation of the bait to the fish. When dealing with a tiny, hard-fished quarry, anglers quickly become accustomed to using hooks from size 20 upwards, but under Irish conditions, at least when pleasure fishing, the angler rarely needs hooks smaller than size 18. The fish are definitely not hook-shy and the majority of fish which you catch will be 2–4oz (60–120g) or more.

There is a huge range of hooks but basically there is one principal division into fine wire and forged. Forged hooks will snap long before they bend but fine wire hooks are more supple and will often straighten if punished by the angler. Fine wire hooks are used for delicate baits while larger baits are normally fished on forged hooks. Shapes are also variable but basically a hook is described as either round bend or crystal bend. Finally, hooks may be divided into eyed hooks and spade hooks. The flattened spade-end hooks are normally tied to lengths of nylon before each fishing session or they may be purchased with nylon or hook-lengths attached. The eyed hooks are attached as required. Hooks are a matter of personal choice and I would advise the novice to sample a range of different types before settling on his own preferred range.

Removing hooks

Since coarse anglers wish to return all fish uninjured to the water they must carefully use a disgorger to remove hooks from the throats of their prey. Modern disgorgers are small aluminium bars containing a very cleverly designed slit and notch. The hooked fish is held in one hand with a slight strain on the line. The disgorger is slipped onto the line via the slit at its tip. It is given a half turn, slid down along the line and gently into the fish's mouth. It slips down over the shank of the hook and is then turned slightly until the eye of the hook is caught in the notch of the disgorger. If you push a little deeper into the fish's throat, the hook slips free and may be quickly removed.

Long-nosed pliers and artery forceps are also used to remove hooks. If the fish is held gently but firmly, even a deeply embedded hook can be removed in seconds.

Big or small, a striped spoon is almost irresistible to a hungry pike

Commercial perch trawling on the rich limestone trout lakes of the Irish midlands. The fish are sold to fund fisheries development programmes (Photo courtesy CFB)

Many anglers have now turned to using barbless hooks which cause less damage to fish and are removed easily. Any hook can be made barbless by simply pinching down the barb with a strong pliers, but be careful not to damage or blunt the point in the process.

Shot and lead

Lead shot

Coarse anglers use both lead shot and bombs. Lead shot may be purchased in separate small containers or in boxes where the various hook sizes are compartmentalised. For the novice coarse angler the latter are by far the best buy since you may instantly choose the correct shot for a given float by matching it to the code on the stem of the float. At times shotting requires that the rig be composed of a range of different shot, the combined weight of which is equivalent to the float rating. This equivalence often confuses people (eg 2AAA = 1 swan) and I have compiled a simplified table outlining some useful comparisons.

1 SSG (Swan)	=	2 AAA
1 AAA	=	2 BB
1 BB	=	2 No.4
1 No.4	=	2 No.6
1 No.6	=	2 No.8

Bombs

I have dealt with bombs briefly under legering but I should add at this point that bombs can be purchased in a variety of shapes. However, the pear-shaped Arlesey bomb with attached swivel is the best variety to choose. Rubber leger stops for use with a running leger rig may also now be purchased.

Present legislation

In England, lead weights are banned because they were found to be environmentally damaging. No such legislation exists in Ireland since we have a much smaller population fishing a much larger area of water. However, the authorities are keeping the matter under review and such a ban may eventually be introduced. If it is instituted, I would imagine that it will only apply to a limited number of heavily fished waters.

Cutting swims

Cutting implements

Except in situations where fishing stands have been erected or along stony shorelines, the angler will be forced to cut his own swim. In richer lakes this will involve not only removing an area of marginal reeds but also the removal of quite appreciable swards of sub-surface plants. I have seen rakes, scythes, light grappling hooks and light chains used for this purpose. Probably the most effective method is the use of two rake heads bound together by wire or strong rope. When forming swims please have some regard for the scenic beauty of the lough or river and remove no more vegetation than is required to make the swim. When you are leaving the swim it is a good idea to cover over its muddied remains with the vegetation which you previously removed.

Plastic covering

If you are planning to fish a given water regularly, semi-permanent swims can be formed by placing sheets of sunken black plastic across chosen marginal areas, in early spring (late February/March). The black plastic blocks the light and stunts plant growth. It only works really well in lakes, for in rivers the plastic may be carried downstream by a flood, regardless of how well you have anchored the sheet. All plastic may be removed in May, for by that time one season's growth has been retarded. Take home the used plastic and destroy it.

Herbicides

In recent years there have also been major advances in the production of selective aquatic herbicides. These are all potentially dangerous substances and their use should only be considered under the most extreme circumstances. Spraying aquatic herbicides is a job for the professionals and the advice and assistance of the local fisheries authority should be sought before attempting to introduce such chemicals into the water.

No.4
SURE-SHOT
BB
NON TOXIC
NON TOXIC
AAA

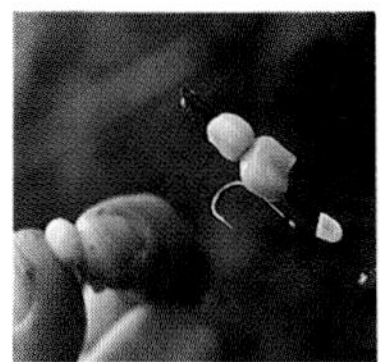

Threading sweetcorn onto a hair rig. The hair is most successful in heavily fished waters, such as Galmoylestown Lake, near Mullingar, Co. Westmeath, which produced this beautifully proportioned brace of young carp

A float for every occasion (well almost!)

KIT

In coarse fishing parlance the kit generally refers to all the articles used to carry the tackle, hold the fish or support the angler!

Box/seat

Most serious coarse anglers equip themselves with a good quality light fibreglass tackle box. These are usually quite large affairs, measuring a half cubic metre or more. The box contains various compartments and a foam rubber seat is normally attached to its lid. Some coarse anglers prefer to carry with them a separate light tubular seat.

Holdall

An array of various float rods, leger rods and pike rods are placed in plastic tubes which are carried in a holdall. It is also used to carry the umbrella, which is placed in a separate compartment attached to the front, and the bank sticks which are placed inside with the rods. A good strong holdall is a most worthwhile purchase for it makes the carriage and storage of all types of rod (sea, coarse and game) so much simpler and safer.

Umbrella

Non-anglers are often amused, and indeed bemused, by the sight of grown men sitting under large green umbrellas along a river bank on a fine summer's day. However, the umbrella is a truly multi-purpose piece of equipment and the angler has no need to apologise for its presence. On fine days it offers a degree of shade and seclusion to the bait, on windy and wet days it provides shelter to the angler and his tackle and during matches it provides the seclusion necessary to change tactics well out of the view of other competitors. On a bad day it may also be used to shelter miserable companions and children, and when the fish are not biting, umbrellas may be put to even more inventive use by young couples.

Keepnet

No angler should contemplate coming to Ireland without a keepnet which is at least 3m long and 0.5m in diameter. Coarse fish are easily damaged in keepnets, particularly bream which are easily haemorrhaged or descaled. Great care should be taken to choose a large keepnet and one made of fine material such as polynet or micromesh. The net should ideally be staked front and back, using strong bank sticks. You may weight the net by carefully placing a stone in the bunt or rear section. Submerge as much of the net as possible and when setting it in a river make sure it is along and not across the current. Unless it is imperative that you weigh your total catch, particularly 80lb+ (36kg) of fish, simply remove the front bank stick at the end of the day and swivel the mouth of the net around until it faces towards the water. Remove the second bank stick and gently tip the fish out of the net. Haemorrhaged or damaged fish are weak and they may either die naturally or fall easy prey to marauding predators.

You should regularly check the keepnet for holes. Micromesh will rot, particularly if stored when damp. Dry your keepnet thoroughly by staking it out in the open air and make sure to shake loose any dried particles of weed, slime or loose scales before storage.

Landing nets

Landing nets should be of a wide diameter (14-18in; 35-45cm) with a long light flexible fibreglass handle. Micromesh should also be used in landing nets. The fish are slipped into the waiting net and it is drawn towards the angler, using the buoyancy of the water to draw the fish towards the bank. Only at the last moment is the rim of the net lifted to the surface. If the angler is properly positioned, he may unhook the fish into the landing net and slip him into the keepnet without having to stand up.

Rod rests

To position leger rods satisfactorily it is necessary to have good quality rod rests. These comprise a bow-shaped metal frame with a pliable plastic tube forming, as it were, the strings of the bow. The rod rest has a screw fitting which slots into the top of a standard bank stick. Bank sticks should ideally be 2½-3ft (80-90cm) in length. Wide rod rests of 12 or 14in (30-35cm) are preferable since they give the angler plenty of manoeuvrability without having to reset the bank stick. Spare bank sticks will be required to anchor the umbrella on windy days and also to hold bait trays or anchor the keepnet.

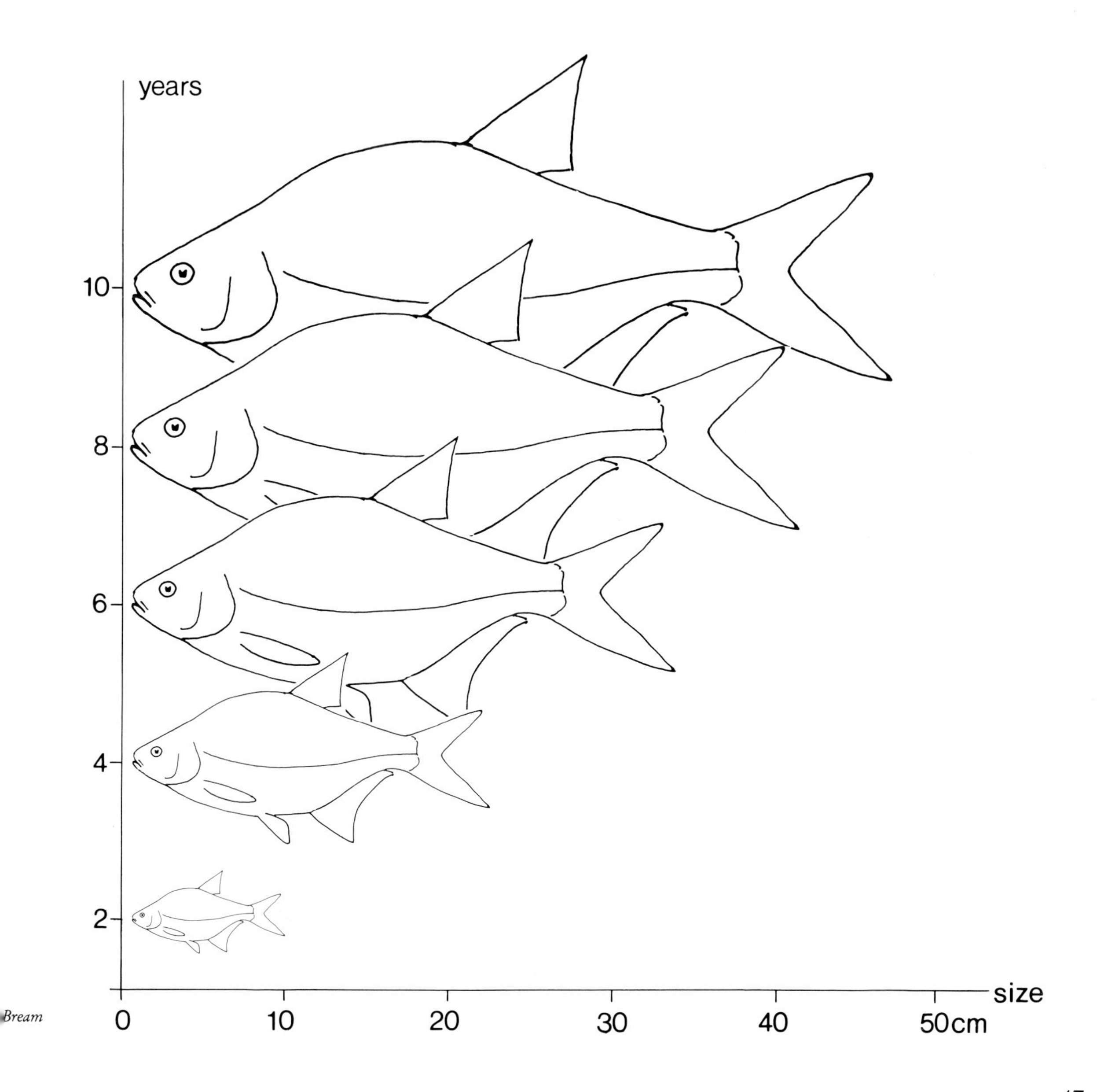

Bream

Stock surveys of rich coarse fish waters frequently involve selective gill netting; such test netting provides a wealth of valuable biological information without damaging the stocks

CHAPTER 4

FISHING FOR CYPRINIDS *Bream and their hybrids*

Life cycle and biology

Growth rates
Bream (*Abramis brama*) are an exceptionally slow-growing shoal fish. The females first mature at seven to ten years of age when they attain the bronze golden coat so characteristic of slab or adult bream. When immature they are silvery in colour and are commonly known as 'skimmers'. In a poor water a bream may have only reached 11in (28cm) at ten years of age, while in rich water a fish of the same age may be 11-16in (28-40cm). They grow to 12lb (5.5kg) or more and can reach an age of twenty-five years. Their main growing season is from May to October and they show an almost complete cessation of growth during the winter months.

Feeding habits
When they first start to feed, bream fry concentrate on tiny phytoplankton and *Aufwuchs,* which are living films of tiny plants and animals found on stones, sticks and plant stems. In this they differ from pike, perch and even tench which are exclusively carnivorous from the start. As the bream grow older they gradually shift to a diet of insect larvae, nymphs, water worms (*Oligochaetes*), shrimp (*Gammarus*), water lice (*Asellus*), caddis and most importantly of all, snails. They are principally bottom feeders but may feed off the lower stems and leaves of marginal vegetation.

In Ireland there is no close season for bream and thus we have an opportunity to observe the behaviour of bream around spawning time. For the angler, this is a particularly difficult period for it provides either the proverbial feast or famine. It is impossible to predict how bream shoals will react at this time. They sometimes feed before the event but both during and immediately after spawning they become unsettled and uninterested in everything bar sex. It is when they return to their feeding areas in early June that they once again seriously consider feeding.

Spawning
Irish bream spawn from mid to late May when water temperatures have reached 13° to 15°C. Mature males are very obvious because of the development of nuptial tubercles on the head, back, shoulders and upper flanks. Male bream stake out a definite spawning territory and aggressively defend this area. Each male spawns with a female or a succession of females, which he pursues through the thicker vegetation in his area. A female bream lays as many as 60 000 eggs per kilogram of body weight. A seven pound (3kg) female could lay 250 000 eggs. In contrast a spring salmon lays 1400 eggs per kilogram of body weight!

Hybrids

The spawning time of bream may overlap with that of both rudd and roach. Cyprinids hybridise more freely than any other family of fishes and all combinations of bream, rudd, roach and tench hybrids have been recorded. However, in Ireland tench spawn at a much later date and natural hybrids have not been recorded. The other extraordinary feature of cyprinid hybrids is that they are often fertile and back-crosses regularly occur. With the current expansion of roach populations throughout our waterways, it is a brave angler indeed who would positively identify hybrids from physical characteristics alone. The only way to be really sure is to test them genetically!

Seasonal movements of bream

One advantage of fishing throughout the spawning season is that it gives biologists an opportunity to tag some of the bream and to learn a little more about their movements. Over a six-year period in the seventies I carried out such a research programme on the River Suck. During the course of the study we tagged 2800 bream, which had been caught by volunteer anglers. From recaptures and also from field observations we were able to deduce some interesting facts regarding the seasonal movements of bream shoals.

The spawning area which we were studying at Derrycahill was used by four distinct shoals of bream. These fish moved into the area during late April and early May and having spawned, the adults moved back to their feeding zones in late May or early June. Spawning migrations took place over as much as a 10km stretch of the river but feeding migrations were much more confined and shoals rarely moved outside of a 2 to 3km home zone. The juvenile and smaller skimmer bream stayed resident in Derrycahill for several years but eventually joined their parent shoal and moved to the adult feeding areas.

We made some estimates of the size of these spawning concentrations and in one year when the four shoals were synchronously gathered in the spawning zone we reckoned there was in excess of 4000 bream present. Some anglers were fortunate enough to encourage part of this massive shoal to feed and one of them, the late Ken Green of Wisbech, had 650lb (300kg) of bream in one sitting. He put so much strain on his back during that particular ten-hour session that the discs eventually locked and he could not move off his basket. Even though he had to be carried back to his van, welded into a sitting position, he vowed it was all 'bloody well worth it'.

Some bream, which we affectionately named 'fliers', migrated distances of 25 to 56km before recapture. These, we are fairly certain, were abnormal movements, possibly associated with fish which had poorly developed homing instincts or fish which bolted due to the presence of the small plastic floy tags in the rays of their dorsal fin. One much celebrated bream decided that being caught

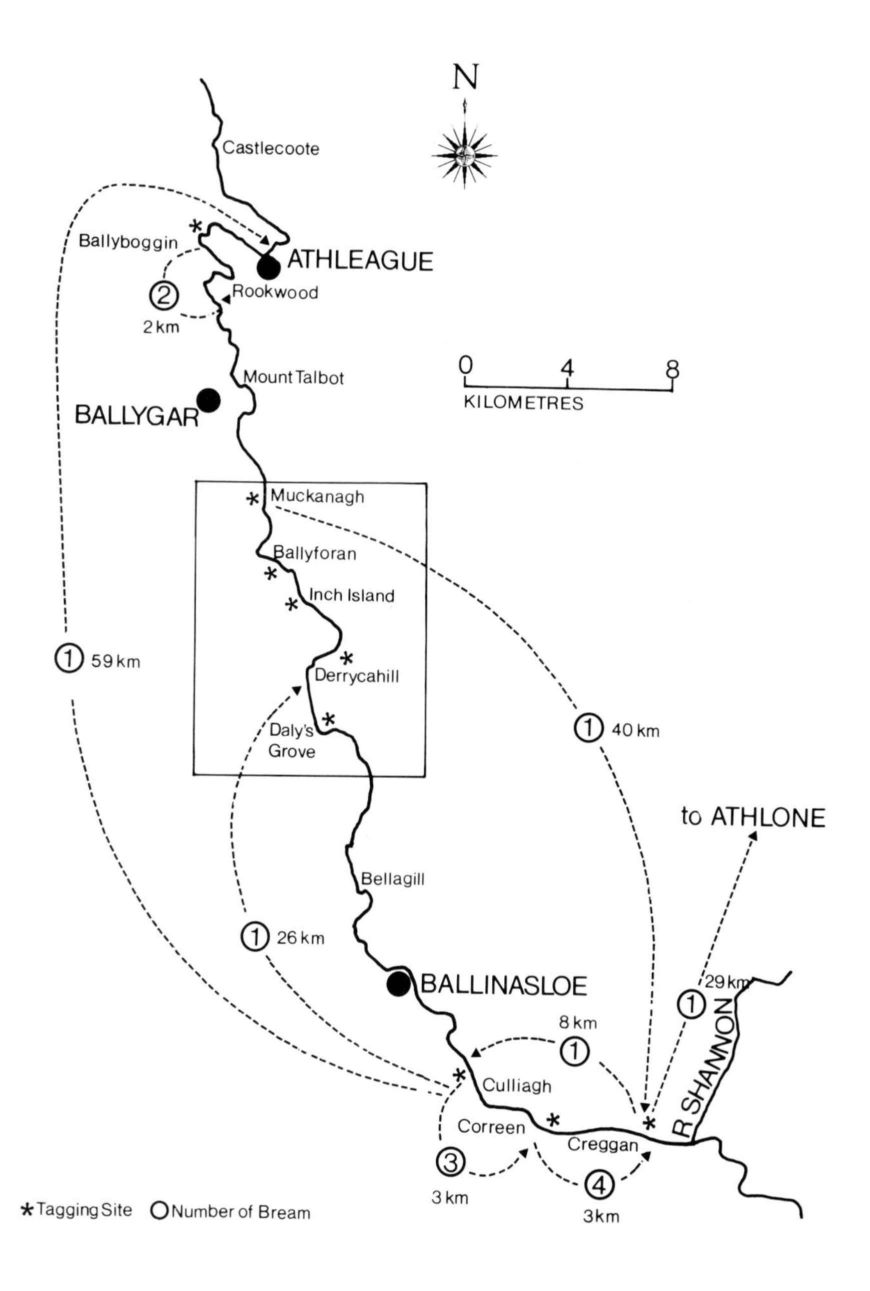

Movement of tagged bream along the Rivers Suck and Shannon

in a single festival (the Ballinasloe Gala) was not quite good enough and so he migrated from the lower Suck into the River Shannon and was caught the following year during the Athlone Bream Festival, a journey of some 29km!

Favourable conditions
Kennedy and Fitzmaurice in their excellent paper on bream, published in 1968, describe what they would consider to be the ideal water for bream in Ireland:

> In lakes the factors which favour rapid growth of bream appear to be high alkalinity; a fair amount of shelter; extensive areas of silty bottom within a depth range of 5 to 20ft [0.5–6m]; and an abundant invertebrate fauna, including big numbers of molluscs, caddis, shrimps and/or water lice, and chironomid larvae. The water should not be so large that it would be difficult to locate the bream shoals; at the same time, it should not be so small that growth-rate would be stunted by over-population. Probably 500 acres [200ha] is the ideal maximum size for a bream water, and 30–50 acres [12–20ha] the minimum [in smaller waters, there is evidence that tench would make better growth than bream]. The ideal bream river is easy to define — wide, deep, slow, alkaline, with a rich invertebrate fauna.

In the context of river fishing for bream it may at times be useful to have some idea of just how slow 'slow' is. During our work on the River Suck we looked into this question and were amazed to find that under low water conditions the current actually appeared to run upstream in the deeper areas. On closer examination we found that these areas were in fact almost static and a strong wind could lead to distinctive movements of the surface layers. The Suck is almost 10m deep in places and we reached the conclusion that the high winter floods have little effect on the deeper water layers. The flood simply pushes out into the extensive flattened floodplain on either side of the river and the surplus water flows gaily along the surface. Although flow rates do marginally increase in the deeper water, the classic, slow, deep bream zone is largely maintained, all year round. A similar situation probably obtains in the Rivers Shannon and Erne, the other two great river fisheries for bream in Ireland.

Fishing for bream

Ground baiting
Bream shoals can, and do, require generous ground baiting. They will readily mop up great mounds of ground bait but for all of that they may be exceptionally fickle eaters. When taking a hook bait they can indulge in a great deal of puffing and blowing before actually sucking the bait down hard. Cyprinids have no teeth in their jaws and their food is masticated in a series of strong vicious-

looking teeth lying deep in their throat, called the pharyngeal teeth. Some authorities on bream angling maintain that the only way to guarantee a solid take from a bream is to ensure that the fish senses a firm, even resistance when he attempts to suck in the bait. The theory is that his initial unsuccessful attempts to lift the bait by sucking will result in a more positive final effort and a firm take; hence the success of running leger or quivertip techniques.

Once bream have settled on your ground bait it is important that you estimate the size of the feeding shoal. Some bream specialists recommend laying the ground bait in a diamond-shaped pattern to accommodate the larger shoals. This advice is often worthwhile but not before you have assessed whether the shoal is big or small. If it is small, the fish may disperse in or around the individual heaps of ground bait and you may find it difficult to locate individuals. I would suggest that you initially ground bait one area and once the fish arrive, test fish within 10 or 20m upstream and downstream. If you continue to contact fish, then you can delicately feed the outer perimeters of the shoal. When bream fishing, it is often intelligent ground baiting rather than sophisticated techniques which make the difference between success and failure.

When leger fishing to either a swingtip or quivertip the angler should not simply cast out the bait and leave it at that. Bream bites can often be induced by twitching the bomb along the bottom, a few yards at a time, every three to five minutes. Remember that bream are often feeding over very soft sediments and once the bomb has settled into the mud, it may draw the hook bait into the finer upper sediments and out of view of the bream. By moving the lead the angler will create a disturbance that I often visualise as a puff of mud, which attracts the attention of the bream and keeps the bait exposed.

Choosing the bait

The bream's preference for various baits may also vary from day to day and the angler is well advised to test a variety of baits. In this way, valuable time may be gained in deciding the bait of the day. Bream will take a whole variety of baits but under Irish conditions it is hard to beat the common worm. As mentioned previously, I have found most success with either brandling, or best of all, redworms. Cocktails are superb and my own favourite is a worm/caster combination.

For night fishing in summer, I prefer bread, either flake or paste. Bream are principally night feeders and the months of June and July, with a low settled river, will provide unsurpassed sport. Bites may be sensed by attaching a night-glowing Betalite tip to your quiver or springtip or by directing a torch beam towards a butt-mounted bite indicator. If you are careful, you need have no fear of frightening the fish for they are often located in 15ft (4.5m) or more of water at a distance of 60–80m from the shore.

Choosing the venue

Anglers visiting Ireland for the first time are often perplexed by the array of different venues available to them within a confined geographical area. The temptation is to try a range of waters until a hotspot is located. In general I think this is the wrong approach. The visiting angler must constantly remember two important factors regarding Irish coarse fisheries. Firstly, they are naturally very rich in food, and secondly, they are relatively little fished. The angler should, therefore, carefully choose a venue, based on angling maps and/or local information and stick to it for at least three to four days.

Float fishing

Bream are also readily taken when float fishing and both the waggler and the slider can be highly effective at taking choosy fish (see page 156). In lakes the standard slider techniques as described in Chapter 3 are ideal but in rivers the use of a slider involves some modifications.

It has been my experience that, at times, bream shoals may lie off the bottom and that at such times layered ground baiting, as practised by the pole fishermen, and the use of a very slow sinking slider bait are essential. Why bream lie off the bottom I do not know for sure but Bill Bolton, who first demonstrated this fact to me on the River Suck, at Ballyforan, County Roscommon, maintained that the bream were following either a temperature or an oxygen gradient. His technique was to feed the fish with semi-buoyant slow-sinking ground bait and to fish up from the bottom by readjusting his slider until he located the position of the shoal. A long tail and bulk shotting ensured that the bait dropped slowly and could be intercepted on its way towards the bottom. Rudd may prove a nuisance at times using this technique but during a match they are a welcome nuisance.

Slider fishing in rivers may be further complicated by the strange flow patterns described earlier. You may find that your float is edging upstream with the wind-blown upper layers of water while your bait is being drawn along by the bottom layers. If the wind is not too strong, you may overcome this problem by adjusting the shot well down the rig so that the upstream movement is compensated for and the float either remains static or slowly follows the bait downstream.

Rudd/bream and roach/bream hybrids behave very much like adult bream. They are principally bottom feeders and will respond well to a generous helping of ground bait. They may be taken on either leger or float tackle but are generally taken on the leger. Large congregations may gather at spawning time and some exceptionally large weights are taken in April and May each year. However, like the bream, these fish are fickle at spawning time and although exceptional catches are made there is nothing consistent about the fishing and one would need to be living on the spot to take full advantage of these spawning shoals.

Rudd

Life cycle and biology

Origin

The rudd *(Scardinius erythrophthalmus)* is, without doubt, one of the most handsome of our freshwater fish; its full golden flanks and the contrasting scarlet of its fins give it a truly exotic appearance. But the rudd is something of an enigma for it is the one cyprinid whose arrival in Ireland remains undocumented and unknown. It is assumed that following the Norman conquests, both it and the bream were imported simultaneously and that because, at the time, it was considered the lesser of the two species, little attention was paid to its arrival.

Whatever its mode and time of arrival, it is a most welcome guest. The rudd is a true stillwater species and shuns large exposed lakes and the faster rivers. Although easily removed from a water by netting or trapping, it is quite a hardy little fish and can tolerate lower oxygen concentrations than many other cyprinid species. However, unlike the tench or carp, it quickly dies if removed from water. It can also tolerate quite a range of salinity and is found in large numbers in the estuaries of both the River Inagh in County Clare and the Owenavorragh River, County Wexford.

Growth rates

Rudd, like the bream, are long-lived, slow-growing fish. In richer waters they may reach 12in (30cm) at ten years of age but in stunted populations fish may have attained no more than 6in (15cm) at the same age. Stunted populations generally occur in small water bodies where overpopulation leads to a premature cessation of growth. Very often such populations are struck by the trematode skin parasite known as black spot (*Posthodiplostomulum cuticola*). This parasite has a rather complicated life cycle involving two hosts, a snail as a primary host and a heron as a secondary host, before finally infecting the rudd. It is not hard to visualise how the trematode appears in stunted populations. The heron, always eager for a relatively easy feed, spots the small clear fish-laden shallow pond and quickly becomes a regular visitor. From its droppings the parasite quickly finds its way into the water and finally into the fish.

Irish rudd grow to 3lb (1.5kg) or more but a 1½lb rudd is considered a good fish and anything over 2lb quite exceptional. The bigger rudd are generally the older individuals which have benefited from accelerated growth in their earlier years.

Spawning

Rudd mature at three to four years of age. They spawn during warm, calm weather from mid-May to early June; when water temperatures have reached 15°C. The males, at times, form loose territorial

Rudd

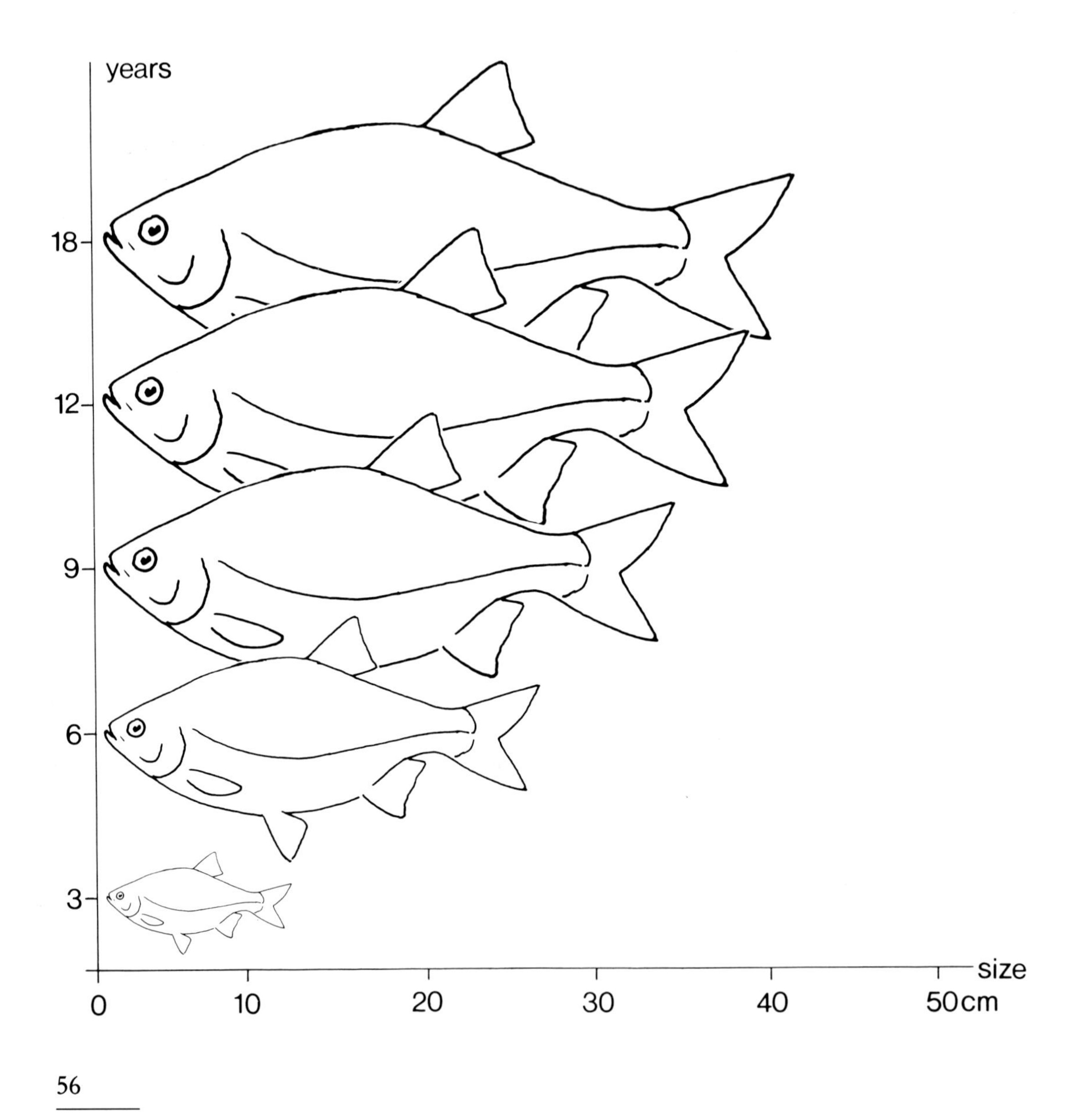

claims but their spawning activity is intermediate between that of the bream, where defined territories are staked out, and the tench where territoriality does not seem to enter into spawning behaviour. Irish rudd have a high fecundity rate and 100 000 to 200 000 eggs per kilogram are not uncommon. A 4oz (113g) rudd may therefore lay between 12 000 and 20 000 eggs.

Feeding habits

The rudd is a perfectly designed surface feeder and its protruding lower jaw ensures that it can easily graze the surface layers of water. Its preferred habitat is the shallow, weedy margins of lakes and slow-flowing rivers. The young rudd fry feed almost exclusively on unicellular algae and only at a later stage do they move onto zooplankton such as the *Cladocera*. The adults are truly omnivorous and feed on a variety of surface insects, caddis larvae, pupae and adults, shrimp, water lice, filamentous algae and vascular plants. The rudd does not ordinarily feed on the bottom and when caught on static baits it is the ground bait which has encouraged the fish to feed at that level.

Because of their surface-feeding habits, rudd attract predators such as pike and at times large trout. To compensate for this fact they are never too far away from cover and shoals quickly disperse once a predator appears on the scene. For that reason, float fishing for rudd, in waters where pike are present, normally occurs in bursts of five to twenty minutes' duration. Once your swim goes dead, lob out a pike bait and more often than not you will succeed in hooking the offender. If you prefer you may wait until the pike has appeased his hunger and moved on. The rudd will then reappear in the swim until another hungry pike arrives on the scene.

Rudd feed consistently from May until October. Outside of this period feeding is erratic, although a mild period, even in mid-winter, can bring them onto the feed. Again, their feeding behaviour may be described as intermediate between the bream and tench which cease to feed in winter and the roach which actively feed all winter long.

Reports from Irish waters where roach populations are expanding indicate that rudd populations are hardest hit by this invasion. This is rather surprising since the rudd and roach would seem to occupy a different but complementary ecological niche; the rudd is mainly a surface feeder, while the roach is principally a mid-water or bottom feeder. The roach's success is largely due to its exceptionally high fecundity and its ability to colonise both flowing and still waters. They seem basically to outbreed the rudd; their year-long feeding season and the fact that fertile rudd/roach hybrids are readily produced in nature has doubtless helped in the roach's apparent conquest of traditional rudd waters.

For a pen picture of the ideal Irish rudd water, we can again turn to the definitive paper on the species, produced by Kennedy and Fitzmaurice in 1974.

(a) Alkaline lakes of 100 to 500+ acres [40-200ha], of fair depth and with adequate marginal weed cover. Such lakes provide excellent fishing for big rudd and also for big bream and big tench.... They are probably the ideal type of lake for good, varied coarse fishing.
(b) Alkaline lakes of 50 to 100+ acres [20-40ha], mostly very shallow and with sparse marginal weed growth, but with occasional deep holes, with belts of bulrushes and other emergent vegetation near the drop-off. These lakes usually provide excellent fishing for big rudd, but are not very suitable for bream.

Fishing for rudd

Surface fishing
Most anglers associate rudd with warm, bright summer days. While rudd can be caught under such conditions they rarely produce big specimens. A mild, overcast evening with a light, tweedy ripple is ideal for big rudd. The ripple gives you that extra cover and makes the larger fish a little less shy.

Since rudd are principally surface or sub-surface feeders, they are mainly taken on various forms of float tackle or on floating baits. The normal procedure is to loose-feed by catapult with small quantities of maggots, floating casters or soft semi-buoyant ground bait. Rudd are shy fish, particularly the really big ones, and any undue disturbance can ruin your chances. Surprisingly, they are not tackle-shy and 3-4lb (1.5-2kg) nylon and size 12 to 14 hooks can be used with confidence. If you think your swim contains rudd, before you have started to ground bait try to find an alternative site for your keepnet, or better still return the rudd caught to the water. It does not seem to disturb the shoal provided you slip the fish back in gently. Try to face the fish into the reeds and he will invariably bolt for cover while he recovers from the shock.

Surface fishing for large 2lb+ (1kg) rudd is one of the most exciting experiences any angler could hope for. I find it difficult to decide whether large rudd shoal or not. They certainly arrive in small groups, but I have a feeling that they are primarily loners. I well remember my first encounter with really large rudd. It was on a shallow backwater of the River Shannon at Shannonbridge, County Offaly. Encouraged by our good friend Derry Kileen, we had decided to fish this secluded bay where he swore the Irish record resided. I do not exaggerate when I say that we encountered at least half a dozen rudd in excess of 2lb (1kg) on that particular evening. Our best fish was a mere 1¼lb (570g) tiddler but our floating bread-flake baits were regularly inspected by 2lb + (1kg) fish. They were rising freely to a hatch of large sedges but none of us had thought of bringing a fly rod.

Leger fishing
Under very weedy conditions rudd may be taken on floating stem legers. These ensure that the line and buoyant bait is held well clear of the bottom vegetation. Leger fishing may also prove

effective in situations where your bank is bereft of weeds but the opposite bank has a strong growth of vegetation. I once saw Ivan Marks, the famous British coarse angler, take over 50lb (22.5kg) of small rudd in a four-hour match using a leger rig and a long 6ft (2m) tail. Fishing single maggot at a distance of 70 to 80m he caught rudd after rudd on the drop. His uncanny ability to sense the slightest twitch of the quivertip as the dropping bait was intercepted, on its pathway through the marginal weed, was a pleasure to behold. All of the rudd were very small 5-8in (13-20cm), but they provided him with a valuable section win.

Bait

Rudd will take a variety of baits including bread, maggot, caster and well-soaked swollen pet food, but the one bait they are not over-fond of is worm. Even on a float they show a clear preference for the maggot or caster. Floating bread may be free-lined or, if distance is required, you could use a self-cocking float. Thread the line through the top aperture and this will ensure that the bread is not pulled under. The red tip of the float is easily seen and you should strike as soon as it moves laterally or disappears. Small 1cm diameter pieces of crust or flake are sufficiently large for most rudd, but if really big fish are present try a large bait. If you decide to grease your cast with a floatant, leave at least 6in (15cm) free of grease just above the hook; otherwise the rudd may notice drag as the line is pulled along the surface. Remember, delicacy in presentation is the key to success when searching for really large rudd.

Fly fishing

Fly fishing for rudd is really great fun and is an excellent way to introduce a beginner to the sport. Most books recommend a dry fly but in my experience daytime fishing is far more productive with a size 14 to 16 nymph. I normally use an Olive Nymph or a Pheasant Tail nymph. I grease the cast but as in the case of floating bait, I leave the last 6 to 12in (15-30cm) free of floatant. A slight breeze is a great advantage and the fly is worked slowly through the shoal of rudd. The take is rather peculiar; the rudd comes towards the fly, hovers for an instant, then sucks it in. You must give the fish plenty of time before striking. The main line is a good bite indicator and when it gives a tremor or a jump you may raise the rod tip and the fish invariably hooks itself.

The dry fly really comes into its own on calm, warm evenings, but again I would suggest that you fish rather small flies: a size 12 Brown Sedge or a size 14 Spent Olive are ideal. A standard dry-fly tapered cast is used ending in a 3 or 4lb (1.5-2kg) point and this is attached to a size 5 or 6 floating line and a light 8ft (2.5m) river fly rod.

BREAM FISHING TECHNIQUES

It is a beautiful warm evening in late June as Paul and I make our way towards the steeply shelving river bank. We are on a section of the middle River Suck known as the Derrycahill bends and are pre-baiting some swims in anticipation of several days' fishing on our chosen stretch. The Suck at this point is a large, deep, slow-flowing river, meandering from right to left through a series of S-shaped soft bends. The river ranges in width from 60 to 80m and shelves to an incredible 10m at some points; the average depth is approximately 5 to 7m.

The bends are used as a spawning site by at least five separate shoals of bream, but by this time of the year only one large resident adult shoal and hordes of smaller juvenile skimmer bream are present.

Our ground bait consists of 70 per cent brown and 30 per cent white bread crumb. To this we have added 1 litre of large casters and approximately 250ml of smaller maggots; a liberal dressing of chopped worm completes the mix. Ground bait is added carefully to the water until we achieve a moist but firm consistency. A few small trial balls of ground bait are formed, and using a whopper dropper they are launched as near to the far reeds as possible. The balls plop into the water unbroken and we know we have achieved the desired consistency.

We are primarily planning to catch large slab bream and so a liberal pre-baiting is required. Bream have great appetites and will readily mop up even the most lavish donation of ground bait. As we prepare a series of large balls of ground bait, Paul and I reminisce about a short-lived innovation which appeared on the banks of the River Suck during one of the gala competitions. Some English anglers, frustrated by their previous inadequate efforts at ground baiting the far margins of the river, had conceived a catapult to beat all catapults. It consisted of a large forked metal frame which was sunk into the soft peat banks. Two extra strong and long lengths of elastic were connected to the extremities of the forks at one end and to a super-large 8in (20cm) diameter cup at the other. The cup of the 'stand-alone' catapult was capable of holding 6in (15cm) diameter ground bait bombs which, if the operator was strong enough, could be fired over 100m. While the super-catapults did achieve their principal aim of firing large balls of ground bait long distances, the resultant disturbances did little to enhance their owners' chances of success in catching bream.

We hand launch our 4in (10cm) diameter balls of ground bait, some 30 to 40m out towards the centre of the river. As far as possible we attempt to concentrate the ground bait into a 2m square area. Each of us uses 5 to 6lb (2.5kg) ground bait during our pre-baiting session. We then mark the chosen swims using a carefully placed twig or stone.

Some anglers would use 14 to 20lb (6–9kg) of ground bait when pre-baiting, but it has been our experience over the years that much smaller quantities are equally efficient at weaning the bream onto the bait.

Morning

The following morning it is a good deal cooler and a faint low mist hangs over the tops of the marginal reeds and rushes. Heavily laden with our full kit, we struggle towards our pre-baited swims, anxious that rival anglers may have inadvertently stumbled upon our chosen venue. Thankfully the banks are clear and we settle down to preparing for the day.

The umbrella is set facing upstream and all the ancillary items of tackle are laid out within its cover. Additional ground bait, similar to that fed on the previous evening, is mixed and 3–4in (8–10cm) diameter balls are added to the pre-baited zone. The river is left to settle while I prepare my leger rod.

I am using a 10ft (3m), fast tapered, medium to full action, fibreglass rod, which is capable of casting a ½ to 1oz (14–28g) bomb considerable distances. My reel is filled with 150m of 6lb (2.5kg) main line, and my cast consists of a 4lb (2kg) line. I choose a fixed leger rig and attach a ½oz (14g) Arlesey bomb and size 8 hook. Onto this is attached a worm/caster cocktail. I carefully place my two rod rests so that the 12in (30cm) swingtip which I am using will form an approximate 45° angle with the flow of the river.

I cast some 40m and wait until the bomb has touched bottom; the tip goes slack and I reel in the surplus line until I am in contact with the settled bomb. I lower the rod onto the two rod rests and set the tip taut just above the water's surface.

Within seconds the tip begins to twitch almost imperceptibly; I cannot believe my luck. The tip straightens; I lift the rod and strike into a good bream. As I sense the heavy throbbing I call to Paul who signals his congratulations — but the fates have a different view. Anxious to land the first fish, I apply strong pressure and seek to haul the fish unceremoniously towards me. Unfortunately, the large bream applies an equal and opposite pressure and the inevitable happens — the hook pulls free.

Disappointed, but with renewed confidence, I re-bait and cast towards the same location. One hour and three small perch later I am still waiting for my bream shoal to return, for I can only conclude that my clumsy attempts at landing the first fish have spooked the settled shoal. Despite all my best efforts and several changes of hook bait, I am still breamless a further hour later.

Paul, on the other hand, has managed to take two good three-pounders and several small skimmers and rudd/bream hybrids. He is also fishing a suspended rudd dead bait as he saw a heavy pike move in a neighbouring bay just as he was preparing his swim.

I decide to go rudd fishing and to rest my bream swim until after lunch. Before leaving, I add several extra balls of ground bait. I leave most of my kit at base camp but gather together some rudd tackle, bait and my keepnet.

I make for a small, heavily weeded backwater, some 100m downstream from the bends. Leaving my tackle on the bank and keeping well back from the water's edge, I throw small portions of white bread crust onto the surface near my own bank. The floating crust has only travelled a short distance downstream when eager, greedy little knebs appear, sucking at the floating morsels. I have located my rudd shoal. I quickly add two or three catapults of loose squatts and maggots and several very tiny balls of soft, extremely wet, ground bait which disintegrate on impact and form a heavy, cloudy suspension in the water.

I have chosen a 13ft (4m) fibreglass float rod, closed-face reel, 3lb (1.5kg) main line and a 3AAA waggler float. I have the float set shallow (approximately 10m; 25cm) and the bulk shotting ensures that the single maggot bait on a size 16 hook falls slowly through the water column.

I wade to the edge of the rather steep ledge, place my bait tray (mounted on a bank stick) and keepnet in position. The float lands with a gentle splosh. It hardly has time to settle before it dips and slides under. I lift the rod and reel in a beautiful golden 6oz (170g) rudd. Several more follow in quick succession. Periods of frantic activity alternate with slack periods for the next hour or more. By this time, I have taken about 10lb (4.5kg) of rudd ranging in size from several ounces to almost a pound. I am really enjoying myself.

As I swing in yet another fish the water explodes and with a sickening lunge the float rod is bent in two. A large pike has seized the rudd and is making for the centre of the river. I pull as hard as I dare to discourage the pike, but he hangs on tenaciously as he strips more and more line from the slipping clutch. Suddenly he drops the bait and, knowing what is coming next, I lift the float rod high and pull the maimed rudd towards me along the surface. The pike, a beast of 12 to 15lb (5.5–6.5kg), has no time for uncooperative prey and lunges at the fast disappearing rudd with such power and ferocity that he engulfs the fish and snaps the thin hook-length in one movement. Thankfully the main line broke below the bulk shot and the waggler is still in place.

I assume that the appearance of the pike and the ensuing commotion has put pay to rudd fishing for quite a while and so, having returned my catch to the water, I make my way back towards Paul's swim. He has had two small bream and a fine 12lb (5.5kg) pike on his suspended dead bait. While we are chatting, I notice a small swirl near the reeds and throw a few crumbs of crust in its direction. To our surprise, a really good rudd surfaces to suck them down. I crimp a small pellet of bread paste onto the size 16 hook and cast towards the fish. The float settles and suddenly slides sideways in a most determined fashion. I lift the rod and feel the firm resistance of a good fish. My prize is a plump red-finned 1lb 10oz (740g) rudd; a real bonus fish.

Afternoon

After lunch, I settle down to some serious bream fishing. My original worm/caster cocktail is replaced by a double maggot/single caster bait on a size 14 hook. After about twenty minutes, the tip gives a slight tremor. I have been moving the bait along the bottom and I know the bomb is now quite close to the steep shelf of my own bank. I let the bite develop and sure enough, the tip eventually swings determinedly. I lift and strike. It is a good fish and after a minute or so of pumping the fish up over the ledge, he is ready for the net; a fine 4lb (2kg) bronze bream.

I cast again and as the tip settles it begins to move up and down, up and down, in an almost rhythmic motion. These are line bites caused by large bream brushing off the nylon as they move through, or hopefully into, the swim. The line bites continue for several minutes, a sure sign of a really good shoal of fish.

Ten minutes later the bream have settled and the fun really begins. Large bream come to the bait on almost every cast for the next two hours and despite bites missed and several dropped fish, I manage to net a very respectable 40lb (18kg) of bream.

Towards evening the wind begins to rise and I am forced to replace the swingtip with a smaller, more wind-resistant, quivertip. With the changing conditions, the bream go off the feed.

Paul's swim continued to produce a steady trickle of good fish throughout the afternoon but he was denied the frantic activity which came my way. I am ready for dinner and a good evening's rest but Paul suggests that we return late in the evening to try some night fishing. Given the day's results, he is certain that fishing after dark will produce an even better return of fish.

Night-time

At around 9.00 pm we arrive back at the swims; less lavishly equipped but with sufficient bait to last us well into the night. Before leaving we had baited the swims with the original ground bait and a small quantity of bread paste. Paul chooses to leger with flake, while I persist with paste.

Because of the soft nature of the bait I change to a running leger and a short 2ft (60cm) trace. I will need immediate contact with the bait if I am to avoid bream sucking off the paste without being hooked.

Ten minutes later I am still without a bite. I decide to change baits and to revert to bread at dusk. A worm/maggot/caster cocktail gives me two excellent bream and a beautiful plump, golden 2¼lb (1kg) rudd/bream hybrid. At dusk I remove my swingtip and set out a simple, bright, white butt indicator, lit by the beam of a strong lamp. I cast my bream bait out into the darkness, set the rod and wait. Less than two minutes pass before the butt indicator lifts decisively. I strike immediately and am rewarded by the deep throbbing of a good fish. Bite after bite follows and despite missing at least six fish out of ten, I still manage to land a good 30lb (13.5kg) of bream. By midnight I am really shattered and, having admired my catch, I slip the fish back into the river.

From somewhere in the darkness Paul shouts excitedly and as I make my way towards his swim, I see his long rod arched in the soft glow of the partially hidden moon. Through the still air I can detect the high-pitched whine of his taut vibrating line. He has hooked a really good bream and needs some assistance. With the aid of Paul's torch and his large diameter net, I manage to land the bream safely and bring him ashore. It is a beautifully proportioned creature, more black than brown, with a broad, high back. It deflects Paul's scales to almost 7lb (3kg), a truly excellent Suck bream and a fitting conclusion to a most fruitful day's fishing.

Roach

Life cycle and biology

Colonisation of Irish catchments

The initial entry of roach (*Rutilus rutilus*) into the River Erne in the 1960s is thought to have occurred as a result of the opening of a drain from Galbally Lough in County Fermanagh, which had been stocked with roach from the Munster Blackwater by a Captain Grosslen in 1931. The rapid spread of roach throughout other catchments in the country may, however, be largely attributed to sport anglers who used the fish as live bait for pike and frequently discarded their surplus bait and to the intentional stocking of roach into various waters by well-meaning groups of coarse anglers. These practices still continue today despite legislation banning the unauthorised movement of live fish.

The successful colonisation of Irish catchments by the roach and its ability to out-compete the resident coarse and game fish stocks may also be attributed to its prolific spawning capabilities, its tolerance and its innate adaptability. The arrival of the roach on the Irish angling scene has certainly heralded change, but whether this change is for the long-term good or detriment of freshwater angling continues to be hotly debated.

Game anglers point towards the closure of Lough Derravaragh, County Westmeath, as a trout fishery and the potential threat which the roach poses for the many excellent trout fisheries on the Shannon, Boyne and Liffey catchments. Roach are now so abundant in Lough Derravaragh that even freshwater trawling had to be abandoned when it was found that the boats were in danger of sinking under the strain of some catches — such trawls can handle a quarter of a tonne of perch with relative ease! An expanding roach population quickly becomes so prolific that it is impossible to reduce or eliminate it by either netting or electrical fishing.

Coarse anglers would, with some justification, point to the Munster Blackwater, where roach and dace have been present since 1889. There, both the salmon and trout stocks appear to be in a healthy condition. The roach and dace may affect angling for brown trout but we have no proof that they cause an actual reduction in salmonid production. There were also claims that rudd and bream stocks declined in the Erne as a result of expanding roach populations but it now seems that the roach populations are stabilising and that the bream, at least, are showing a welcome reappearance in anglers' catches.

The benefits which roach have brought to Ireland are immense. They have resulted in increased tourist angling revenue and have also provided the basis for winter, autumn and early spring coarse angling matches. The expanding populations have provided fish of extraordinarily high average size and bags of 500lb (230kg) or more during a four-hour match have been recorded on the Rivers Bann and Erne. Roach have also appeared in large number in the two major canals in Dublin — the Grand and Royal Canals. Recent survey work has shown the presence of 5000 roach in a 5km stretch of the Grand Canal within the city limits. Such fisheries provide ideal 'nursery areas' for budding anglers. The expansion of the fodder fish base in the larger waters has also greatly benefited the predatory fish such as pike and ferox trout. The recent discovery that the oily nature of the roach made it an ideal ray bait has further stimulated the interest of sea anglers in the species!

In biological terms, the roach invasion, even that of the Munster Blackwater, is a very recent event. It will take time for the new species to follow the classic invasion sequence of population expansion, contraction and stabilisation. The roach will ultimately find its ecological niche in Irish waters but this may take a further century or more. Let us hope that when it finally completes its adaptation that we will be the richer for its presence and that we do not have to sacrifice in its favour any of the other resident species.

Growth rates

The roach's ability to dominate a catchment in such a short period of time is based on an exceptionally high fecundity rate and maturation at a young age. Research work on roach from the River Annalee, County Cavan, has shown that both the males and females mature at three years of age. The minimum size at maturity for males can be as low as 3in (7.5cm), while females may mature at 4in (10cm). However, if growth is faster and these critical lengths are attained earlier, maturity may be reached at two years of age, at least in the males.

Growth rates are, at present, highly variable and in expanding populations which inhabit rich waters, roach may reach 9in (23cm) at four years of age. On the continent and in the UK it would take, even under suitable conditions, seven to twelve years for them to reach 10in (25cm). In contrast, settled populations of roach in the River Annalee average 6–7in (15–17cm) at five years of age. Roach are generally regarded as a slow-growing fish, but they often live to fifteen or more years of age. As mentioned previously, they readily hybridise with both bream and rudd and such hybrids are fertile. This results in various permutations and combinations of first and second generation back-crosses.

Spawning

The fecundity or egg-laying capacity of roach is truly exceptional. For instance, a 14oz (400g) fish was found to contain 136 000 eggs. At one spawning site on the River Annalee it is estimated that over 270 million eggs were laid in an area 80 to 90m^2! This is equivalent to a fecundity of 300 000 eggs per kilogram of body weight.

In Ireland, roach generally spawn between May and mid-June, when water temperatures have reached at least 13° to 15°C. They prefer a stony or gravel bottom covered with dense submerged vegetation. They are often found spawning in glides where the flow rates are between 0.6 and 1 m/sec. and where there is a luxuriant growth of *Ranunculus* and *Phalaris* spp. Roach do, at times, spawn in lakes but seem to prefer to do so in the inflowing or outflowing rivers.

I was fortunate some years ago to witness roach spawning in the River Inny, County Westmeath. Huge shoals of fish had moved upstream from Lough Derravaragh and were concentrated into marginal areas of the river. Spawning took place late in the afternoon and the boisterous and at times aggressive ritual continued well into the evening. There were such concentrations of fish present that some females actually emerged from the water and flipped and flopped their way along the marginal vegetation, leaving in their wake a string of shiny adhesive eggs. After several hours, patches of such exposed, and I presume unfertilised, eggs were to be seen glistening like tiny pearls all along the margins of the river. The submerged plants were themselves coated in a thick layer of tiny glutinous eggs. The sheer volume and density of fish present is impossible to describe.

Before spawning, the male roach develops small spawning tubercles along the head, back and flanks. These appear like a fine skin rash. But unlike the bream, where the males alone develop tubercles, a lighter though nonetheless distinctive rash may also appear on the female roach.

Feeding habits

Roach are omnivorous feeders and regularly consume insects, crustaceans, snails, milfoil, duckweed, stonewort and algae. They are primarily mid-water or bottom feeders but are not averse to feeding on the surface.

Seasonal movements

Locating roach shoals can, at times, prove quite a hit-and-miss affair. They are prone to mass movements and may quickly disappear from an area where they were previously in residence for several weeks or even months. It would seem that there are three principal seasonal movements, overlaid by feeding migrations, which would appear to be very variable and ill-defined. Roach, unlike the other Irish cyprinids, feed actively throughout the winter period. In late March or early April various feeding shoals begin to mass prior to the spawning migration. The males make the first move and are often present in the vicinity of the spawning areas well ahead of the females. When spawning is completed in late May or early June the roach migrate towards moderately shallow feeding areas. Classically, such summer locations are to be found near beds of fine gravel or stones where the in-stream vegetation is lush; the typical glyde of the trout angler. Here they remain until mid to late October when they move towards the deeper areas, often feeding for the winter period, just above, or on, a mud bottom.

Fishing for roach

Fishing for roach may be conveniently divided into two major sub-divisions: fishing for the smaller, more prolific roach and fishing for specimen roach over 2lb (1kg). Specimen roach are scarce in Ireland at present but as populations stabilise and densities diminish, I have no doubt that we will see an increasing number of larger roach.

Fishing for small roach

The smaller roach are shoal fish and voracious and competitive feeders. The activities of those first arriving in the swim after ground bait has been added seems to attract hordes of other interested and hungry individuals. Their bush telegraph is second to none. Simple tactics work best for roach and yet again the key to success is intelligent ground baiting.

Even within a swim roach are very prone to move without warning and if your fish suddenly disappear do not assume that they have moved out of the general area. They may have relocated either above or below their original position in the water column. Vary your float rig so that it fishes either deeper or shallower; try fishing on the drop or lengthen the hook length and put on a more buoyant bait. A pike may have entered the area and you must either wait for him to satisfy his hunger or pass a seductive bait past his nose.

Roach are generally taken on float tackle but leger may also be used. Because of their relatively small size and poor fighting qualities you may find it sufficient to fish a light swan leger on 2lb (1kg) nylon.

Ground bait

Roach ground bait is generally very straightforward and many anglers simply use dampened mashed loaf bread mixed with a small quantity of crumb. The crumb helps to bind the small balls of ground bait which are about the size of an egg and which are added sparingly to the swim. Other anglers prefer loose feeding with maggot or caster.

Hook baits are legion and maggot, caster, sweetcorn and stewed wheat are all regularly used. Amongst the more bizarre roach baits are elderberries, pearl barley and even cubes of congealed ox blood! During warm summer conditions hemp is particularly successful as a ground bait, but if not used sparingly it may result in the fish feeding on it to the exclusion of all other baits.

Fishing for large roach

Larger roach are generally quite solitary individuals. As with large rudd, they may move about in small groups but it is not unusual to locate a single large fish. They are great wanderers and their location requires quite a deal of reconnaissance and may only be definable within a general area. In still water they seem to prefer steep ledges, while in rivers they are to be found at the rim of slacks or eddies.

Richard Walker, who over his career caught many hundreds of 2lb+ roach, has defined the three main features of catching big roach as follows:

1. Big roach feed most freely from approximately one hour before until one hour after sunset.
2. A bait lying still on the bottom is more successful than one suspended above the bottom or moving with the current.
3. While there are hundreds of different baits that have accounted for big roach, it is rare to find roach anywhere that refuse either bread, in one form or another, or large worms. This means that if no roach are caught on either of these baits, it is unlikely, though not impossible, that a change to any other bait will succeed. Failure is much more likely to be caused by some other factor.

One of the principal reasons for using large and simple baits such as bread or worms is to discourage the smaller roach. For this reason the angler should be circumspect with his ground bait and limit himself to bread balls. Even large roach are poor fighters and 3lb (1.5kg) nylon may be used with confidence. Hook sizes are generally large — 10s and 12s, or even 8s. When fishing bread, strike at the first signs of a bite, but with worms wait for the bite to fully develop.

Most large roach are taken on a static float rig but a leger may also be used. The strength of the tackle is very much governed by the distance which must be cast and the weights in use, rather than the size of the fish. For really long distance leger casting, a built-in quivertip is a tremendous advantage.

Tench

Life cycle and biology

Introduction into Irish waters

The first recorded importation of tench and carp into Ireland occurred during the reign of James I (1603-25). However, monastic settlements may previously have introduced batches of these fish into Ireland. The tench (*Tinca tinca*) are native to continental Europe and prefer the typical extremes of that climate — exceptionally warm but relatively short summers and long, cold, harsh winters. Tench have adapted well to Irish conditions and despite the vagaries of the weather have truly revelled in the richness of our limestone rivers and lakes.

When hooked, the tench is a strong and determined fighter. As a consequence, it is a much sought after sport fish, particularly in waters where it grows large. To cater for this demand the Inland Fisheries Trust began to survey and stock suitable tench waters in 1956. Since that time more than eighty angling waters have been developed and many hold tench well in excess of the present Irish record of 7lb 13¼oz (3.5kg). While surveying the River Suck I personally trapped and returned a tench which weighed between 11 and 12lb (5-5.5kg). I had no weighing scales with me at the time but an accurate length measurement was taken and later applied to a length:weight growth chart.

When the seed population of tench is first stocked into the chosen water, the classic pattern is for them to 'disappear' for some five to six seasons. Following this slack period tench begin to appear regularly in anglers' catches and if the stocking has been a success, the water acquires a reputation as a tench fishery within a decade after stocking.

The ideal Irish tench fishery is a 50-300 acre (20-120ha) shallow, rich, limestone lake. However, tench populations have adapted exceptionally well to other waters and excellent tench are to be found in the larger midland rivers and also in the rich limestone canals. The Royal Canal, which flows between Mullingar and Dublin, has a particularly fine head of tench of a large average size. The exceptionally clear water offers a unique challenge to the ardent tench angler.

Peculiarities

Tench are an exceptionally hardy fish and may live for long periods out of the water. Once their gills are left moist, by covering them with wet newspaper or wet sacking, they may be transported over relatively long distances. Perhaps the classic example of the durability of tench was cited by

Kennedy and Fitzmaurice in their 1970 paper on Irish tench:

> [A] Specimen [was] sent to the Trust for identification by a fisherman who caught it in a lake where tench were previously not known to exist and who had not seen one before. It arrived by ordinary parcel post the day after despatch. When it was unpacked and was being examined, a slight quivering of its fins was detected. It was placed in a sink full of water, where it rapidly revived. The following day it was liberated in a canal, none the worse for its experience!

Even when damaged by abrasion from nets or traps, the fish quickly recover; hence their reputation as a source of mystical medicinal powers.

Young tench differ from the other cyprinids which we have dealt with so far in that they are almost entirely carnivorous. They first feed on small planktonic forms such as *Cladocera* and *Copeopods*; as adults they feed on a wide range of bottom organisms including snails, midge larvae, caddis larvae, mayfly nymphs and crustaceans. When feeding on such organisms some plant material is ingested but the quantities are small and it is unlikely that the fish intentionally feed on plants.

Tench are an excellent table fish and their soft, delicate flesh is highly regarded in many eastern European countries. In parts of Poland, for example, tench are traditional Christmas fare and are served as a main course on St Stephen's Day (Boxing Day). As with carp, the fish are held in baths of clean water for several days before they are sacrificed; this relieves them of the incipient muddy taste which is present in the freshly caught fish.

Growth rates

Tench are relatively slow-growing. In a rich water a female may reach 16in (40cm) at seven years of age but only 11in (28cm) for the same age in a poor water. Tench may reach 12lb (5.5kg) or more in weight and have a maximum lifespan of twelve or fifteen years.

They mature at three years of age even where conditions are poor; mature tench of only 5in (13cm) have been recorded. After two years the females begin to grow faster than the males and this growth differential is maintained throughout life. Adult tench can be easily sexed. The second ray on the pelvic fins of the male becomes thickened. These fins grow longer in the male and their tips almost reach the vent.

Tench are prone to viral and bacterial dropsy. This may lead to a massive retention of fluid and an unnatural increase in body weight. This condition is also known as 'Red-spot' and appears in the fish as a dense red rash in early spring, immediately after they resume regular feeding. Rod-caught fish suffering from dropsy may result in a new record but a doubt obviously exists as to the validity of such records from a biological point of view.

Tench

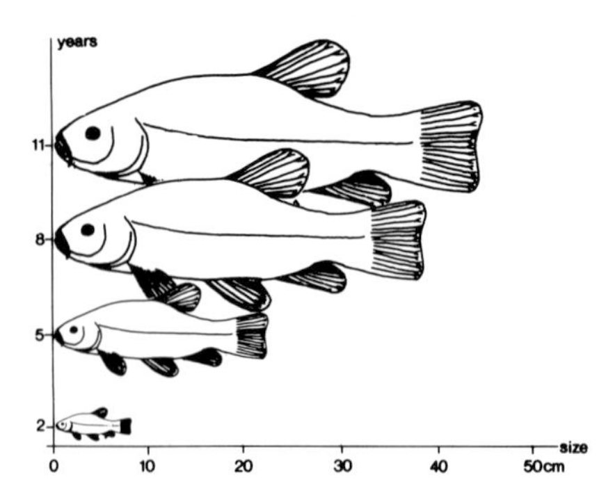

During the autumn tench cease to feed actively and apart from some minor feeding forays during particularly mild spells of weather in winter, they remain dormant until spring. Under Irish conditions, both tench and carp have been found tucked up in rich beds of stonewort during the winter months. When disturbed they gradually became active but were obviously in a deep torpor on the lake bottom before being disturbed. The growth period of Irish tench is quite confined and occurs between mid-May and early October.

Spawning

Tench spawn in late June and July amongst heavily weeded areas of both rivers and lakes. They require a water temperature of 18° to 20°C and really successful spawning is normally consistent with a two- to three-week midsummer anticyclone. The fish form loose spawning assemblies and each female is generally accompanied by two or more attendant males. Females need not wait until they reach the thickest vegetation before releasing their eggs and indeed the spawn may be widely dispersed over the spawning area. The fecundity of tench is exceptionally high and up to 300 000 or 400 000 eggs per kilogram of body weight have been recorded.

Fishing for tench

Tench are primarily dawn and dusk bottom feeders. They are shoal fish and adore heavy concentrations of lily pads. They are often to be found where the shelf drops smartly into two to three metres of water and tench may lie right under the bank. These dense areas of lily pads are frequently described as 'cabbage patches' by coarse anglers.

When tench fishing, always assume that there are tench in your swim and tackle up well back from the water's edge. Feed the swim very gently to start; a dozen or so grains of sweetcorn is often sufficient or in deeper water two or three egg-sized balls of ground bait. Do not lash out your keepnet into the swim but rather find an alternative spot for it; better still, return all tench caught directly to the water. If you slip them back into the reeds, it does little to disturb the remainder of the shoal.

Where the vegetation is particularly dense it may be necessary to cut swims. Using twin rake heads, tied back to back, remove just sufficient instream plants to allow you to fish comfortably. The very act of removing the water weeds will attract tench, for they have a keen sense of smell and the odour of the disturbed river or lake bottom is quickly detected by the marauding shoals.

Pre-bait the swim using plain ground bait. This normally comprises proprietary ground bait, bread crumb, corn and worms — make sure to include a good proportion of your proposed hook bait. The tench will actively dig around the disturbed area and their presence may be detected by the very distinctive bubble pattern which their feeding creates. This appears as intermittent but intensive bursts of fine bubbles. Bream also leave a bubble trail under such circumstances but it consists of a larger, more irregular pattern.

Bait and tackle

Hook baits for tench are legion, but under Irish conditions sweetcorn, worm and maggot are the three favourites. Tench are the strongest of the Irish cyprinids and where large fish are present I would advise 6lb (2.5kg) main line and the use of forged round-bend, eyed hooks, sizes 8 to 10. Smaller or fine wire hooks are easily straightened by the first strong, burrowing run of a tench.

To catch tench, either static float or leger is used. For leger fishing, a running leger is best. As with roach, strike immediately you sense a bite when using soft baits, such as bread and corn, but allow the bite to develop when the bait is worm or caster. A longish, full-action leger rod (10–11ft; 3–3.5m) is generally called for. This allows fish to be held out from the marginal vegetation. To handle large tench, a strong rod is required and it is essential that it have a full action, providing an even bend from tip to butt.

Float fishing is normally carried out using a waggler (see page 155). The lift-bite technique is the most popular method and the float length is set just over depth. Arrange the rig so that the float sinks under the shotting but the tip rises once the hook weight touches the bottom. Strike as the float lifts but if it gyrates from side to side or moves up and down erratically, you may be sure that the tench are playing with the bait. Altering the depth at which the bait is fishing will often result in a firm take.

Although normally regarded as solely bottom feeders, tench may be found mid-water feeding off steep banks or ledges. When they are located along such shelves it is often necessary to rig a mid-water float and fish as tight as possible into the ledge. Tench have even been known to take deep-sunk artificial flies but it is not a method to be recommended!

It is late May and, although the weather forecasts tell us that air temperatures are near to normal, there is a strong hint of north in the predominantly westerly wind. This morning is no exception, and as we arrive at the lake, just before dawn, a nippy force 4 to 5 breeze reminds us that good warm clothing is the order of the day. Considering the air temperature, I am rather sceptical of our chances with the tench but Paul reassures me that water temperatures are well up on average and several good bags of fish have already been taken.

Our chosen venue is Ballyhoe Lakes; two relatively small, 35 and 50 acre (14 and 20ha), kidney-shaped lakes, lying along the Meath/Monaghan border, near the village of Dromconrath. The two lakes are joined at their northern tips by a low-lying marsh, which floods during periods of high water and forms a water bridge. The most productive tench swims are located in the smaller western lake, commonly known as Ballyhoe 1.

We are trudging towards a sheltered, rich, reedy bay, where a minor tributary joins the lough, one of Paul's favourite tench locations and an area which has yielded several specimen tench in excess of 6lb (2.5kg). Eventually we reach the banks of the relatively small but deep and slow-flowing tributary. The bank shears off into quite deep water and is lined with thick swards of vegetation. Ideally, one would set to work with a swim-clearer, but since we do not wish to disturb any feeding tench present, we both choose areas where there are small gaps in the fringe vegetation.

Keeping well back from the bank, I feed several small balls of quite soft ground bait and a handful or two of sweetcorn — my intended hook bait. I assemble my tackle and allow some minutes for the tench to start feeding on the ground bait.

I have chosen to fish a 13ft (4m) fibreglass float rod, a closed-face reel, loaded with 6lb (2.5kg) main line and a 3 AAA waggler float. I carefully plummet the depths directly in front of me and find that it varies between 2.5 and 3m deep, I set the float some 60cm over depth and arrange the shotting so that the float sinks initially but the tip reappears once the bait and single BB indicator shot has settled on the river bed. There is a heavy coating of instream vegetation in places,with patches of lily pad dotted across the surface of the stream, and I am concerned that my bait may sink into the carpet of stonewort. However, I will not know this until I have test-fished the swim. My hook is a size 10 wide-gape, forged hook and the intended hook bait one or two pellets of sweetcorn.

As I watch the inner margins of the stream, I am delighted to see that my patience has been rewarded. Short, intense, hissing streams of fine bubbles appear off the bottom mud, as the hungry tench forage intensely for the partially hidden feed. I move some 10m upstream and gently set my keepnet. I could release all tench caught without disturbing the swim, but Paul and I have a small wager on the best catch of the morning, which I intend to win.

I swing my rig out some 3m from the bank and gently settle down behind the reeds. The float stays motionless for several minutes while all around siphons of tiny intense bubbles move closer and closer to the hook bait. I have just decided that the bait is hidden from view and have reached for the rod when the stationary float sways gently from side to side. Was it my hand touching the rod or was it a definite bite? I wait. The float sways a second time but with a more distinctive motion, and slowly and smoothly it rises until it is floating on the surface. I lift the rod and a strong tench, startled by the sudden resistance, bolts for the nearest clump of lily pads. I am too slow and the fish burrows deep, sending up sprigs and leaves and a stream of fine muddy sediment. I apply as much pressure as I dare, and to my relief the fish bolts out into clearer water.

After a minute or so the tench is ready for the net, but once it sees the rim it summons up one final burst of energy and races for the far bank, a reminder that large, strong fish should never be taken for granted. Eventually, 3½lb (1.5kg) of thick-set, dark green tench are mine. The fish is lip-hooked. I quickly remove the barb and carry the fish in my landing net to the keepnet.

Despite all the commotion, the tench continue to forage and by gently feeding the swim, I manage to hold the fishes' attention for several hours. Two more tench are landed, a three-pounder and a second three-and-a-half pounder. Paul also sees some action to his running leger rig and I estimate that he has four tench, one more than myself. His first fish gave him a long battle and I would not be surprised if it topped 4lb (2kg). The fate of the wager seems in doubt.

As the sun peeps through the cloud for the first time and the wind freshens, the tench show less interest in feeding and the bubble patterns disappear. I change the shot pattern and the depth of the bait several times but fail to connect with any further tench. I change to a leger rig, for Paul has caught two additional fish and he is surging further and further into the lead. I decide on a fixed leger and a long tail, a size 8 hook and a most unorthodox single worm/corn cocktail.

I set my short quivertip close to the water's surface so as to reduce its movement in the strong breeze. But I need not have worried, for when the bite comes it is a strong, positive take. I let it develop and strike, a nice plump 2lb (1kg) tench joins its companions in the keepnet.

It is getting near our predetermined lunch hour and the end of our tench 'match'. I re-bait and drop my bomb near to a heavy clump of lily pads where I had noted a great deal of activity earlier in the morning. The tip remains motionless for almost ten minutes; it then begins to move almost imperceptibly to the left and right. It gives several gentle twitches and then streaks to one side. As I strike, I realise that the fish is a really heavy one. It moves about the bottom of the river with all of the subtlety and power of an out-of-control juggernaut. I call to Paul for some assistance and he races towards me excitedly. With his calming influence and experienced advice, my large tench is soon ready for the net. And what a fish it is — 5¼lb (2.5kg), my largest tench to date. As Paul lands the fish, the local church bells are striking twelve o'clock. Time to compare catches. Paul has six tench, including one four-pounder, giving him a total bag of 17¼lb (8kg). I have five tench and incredibly these also come to a total of 17¼lb. Despite calls for a second weighing, it is impossible to differentiate between the two bags and we decide that the £2 wager should go to charity.

CHAPTER 5

PERCH & PIKE

Perch

Life cycle and biology

Origin

We have no information on when and how the perch first reached Ireland. From its distribution within Europe and the UK and its Irish name, *péirse* — which is an exact derivation of the English name — it is assumed that it is an introduced species. It was probably imported, with the pike, in the sixteenth and seventeenth centuries.

Perch are widely distributed throughout Eurasia, except for the Iberian peninsula, and have been stocked into waters in Australia, New Zealand and South Africa. The European perch (*Perca fluviatilis*) and the North American yellow perch (*Perca flavescens*) are considered different species by most taxonomists. In fact the only obvious difference is in the position of the predorsal bones; in all other behavioural and biological characteristics the two 'species' are exactly alike. As far as the angler is concerned, they may be regarded as the same fish.

Characteristics

The coloration of perch is variable, depending on diet and location, but it is normally a strikingly handsome fish, largely olive green on the back and upper flanks, with a yellow tinge to the lower flanks and ventral surface. The flanks are striped and the ventral and tail fins are bright red. The perch is heavily armoured with a strong row of high dorsal spines, opercular spines and a rough, scaly skin.

Perch are exceptionally difficult to transport from one water to another. It is not clear whether the observed high mortalities are due to stress or to the physical damage which their spines may inflict on one another in transit. For all that, perch are a hardy fish which may withstand temperatures from just above freezing to 31°C and salinities up to $12^{\circ}/_{oo}$. ($^{\circ}/_{oo}$ = measure of salinity in parts per thousand. Normal sea water is $35^{\circ}/_{oo}$.) They thrive in the Baltic where salinities range between $7^{\circ}/_{oo}$ and $10^{\circ}/_{oo}$.

Perch are largely a shoal fish and such shoals are normally stratified by sex, age and size. They are daylight feeders and are most active during the early morning and at dusk. Perch are normally inactive at night. In lakes, feeding shoals form each morning and disperse immediately after dark. In perch populations there are three distinct seasonal migrations: spawning, feeding and over-wintering.

Spawning

Male perch mature at age one or two and females mature one or two years later. The males are the first to reach the spawning ground and may remain in the vicinity until all the ripe females have completed reproduction. Spawning takes place between early April and mid-May at a water temperature of 9°-12°C. When environmental conditions are favourable, spawning may be completed in twelve to fourteen days.

Female perch are attended by groups of males, and as each female releases her characteristically long, hollow, twisted, cylindrical egg strand, the males eagerly set to work fertilising selected sections. An individual egg strand may be 2m or more long and contains an immense number of eggs. Perch release in the region of 150 000 per kilogram of body weight and it has been estimated that in a rich lake as many as two million eggs per hectare are laid.

The spawn is released onto submerged vegetation, bushes and trees. When developing waters as trout lakes the fisheries authorities use this behaviour to control perch numbers. They bind together bundles of branches which are anchored on the bottom during the perch spawning season. Daily servicing results in the removal of millions of perch eggs.

The eggs hatch after eighteen to twenty days and the young fish quickly adapt to a planktonic diet. They form huge pelagic or mid-water shoals which graze the surface plankton. By mid-June they are large enough to attract predators, which include pike, trout and adult perch.

Cannibalism

Cannibalism is common amongst perch from a length of 1in (2.5cm). They are fierce little fish and their jaws are lined with rows of sharp backward-sloping teeth. They are highly aggressive and when faced with an enemy the transverse bars on their flanks disappear, they develop a dull shade of green and arch their backs. They spread wide all of their fins and flair their operculars (gill-covers), revealing the bright red gills and projecting out the strong opercular bones.

In the period June to September each year, harassing shoals of perch fry is the major preoccupation of both adult perch and brown trout. It has been calculated that in Lough Leven (Scotland) perch fry constitute 30 per cent of trout food and 13 per cent of adult perch food for the same period. In fact, adult perch have been known to eat 89 per cent of their own weight of perch fry in four summer months.

Perch populations show particularly strong year-to-year variations in abundance. Such fluctuations are dependent on the strength of a given year-class. A population may be dominated for five or six seasons by a particularly strong year-class; which effectively limits the success of subsequent brood years by cannibalising them.

Perch are not very fast swimmers but have developed a very effective co-operative hunting technique. This ensures that shoals of even the most agile fodder fish may be surrounded and attacked.

Growth rates

Growth rates are highly variable amongst perch populations and are regulated by such factors as the availability of food and the presence of predators. In stunted populations all the fish may be less than 8in (20cm), but in rich waters perch may reach this size at two years of age. Both males and females grow at the same pace until two years of age when the females growth rate increases. This growth differential is then maintained in subsequent years. Perch rarely live beyond ten to twelve years of age.

Adult perch feed on a variety of insects, snails, crustaceans and fish. In the older age groups, fish are progressively more important, but invertebrates are eaten throughout life. Where food is abundant perch may grow to 3lb (1.5kg) in as little as five or six years.

The largest perch ever recorded was 22lb (10kg) but this monster was taken from an Australian water into which perch had been introduced. In the USSR, perch of 7–10lb (3–4.5kg) are regularly taken but in the UK and Ireland perch rarely grow beyond 6lb (2.5kg) in weight. The present Irish record stands at 5½lb (2.5kg).

In Ireland, large lake perch are most common in small to medium-sized, rich, limestone lakes where pike are absent. Such lakes are often quite deep and as a consequence have only a moderate flora. Perch grow fat on the rich invertebrate larder and on a varied fish diet which includes appreciable quantities of perch fry, in season. These are exceptionally fast-growing fish and a three-pounder may be only five to six years of age. Because of the absence of pike, both natural minnow and spinning are very effective baits. My best perch to date (2lb 15oz) was taken on a small silver Toby from one such lake.

Large river perch are not now very common in Ireland, possibly because of arterial drainage. When they do occur they seem to prefer a moderate flow over gravel or stone which is fringed by a heavy growth of reeds and rushes. They are found in the vicinity of shoals of coarse fish fry and according to local information are almost entirely piscivorous (fish-eating). When river fishing, the angler is unlikely to catch a perch much larger than 3lb (1.5kg) but in a rich lake a five-pounder is always a possibility.

Debatable value

It is difficult to say whether, on balance, perch are an advantage or a disadvantage to Irish fisheries. They certainly provide a very effective mechanism for converting invertebrate food into usable form for the top carnivores such as trout and pike. They also provide direct fodder for these species. Perch do, however, prey on the eggs and fry of salmonids, bream, pike and roach. There is also indirect evidence that large stunted populations may so effectively harvest invertebrate production in the smaller limestone lakes, that trout growth is adversely affected.

Fishing options

My first experience of catching perch was in the early sixties, in Lough Ramor, County Cavan. My brother and I were only starting on our freshwater fishing careers and up to that point the most fish we had caught in a single day was three or four. Imagine our delight and excitement when we managed to catch twenty-three perch, averaging about half a pound, in a single afternoon. The fish were subsequently skinned and fillets of their delicious soft white flesh were foisted on friends and neighbours alike. This mammoth catch made a significant impression on us at the time and ever since the catching of perch has rekindled in me a pleasurable feeling of fondness and familiarity.

Perch fishing is a little like roach fishing in that the angler must initially make a choice: is he interested in catching large numbers of small to medium-sized perch (up to 1lb; 450g) or is he seeking the more elusive 2-3lb (1-1.5kg) fish. Really large perch are difficult to locate and although some good fish are invariably present on the perimeter of feeding shoals, I believe that perch over 2lb (1kg) prefer a singular existence.

Bait

Perch are generally not difficult to catch and it is more often a case of them finding you rather than you locating them. Although they are attracted by ground bait, it is not often used by anglers when perch fishing since the odd catapult of loose maggots or chopped worm is more than sufficient to hold a shoal of perch. They are tenacious feeders and will circle round and round an area searching for hidden morsels long after the loose feed has been gobbled up by the shoal.

Perch will take a whole variety of baits including worm, maggot, caster, minnow, spinner, plug and fly. Worm is the most common bait and it is generally fished on a simple waggler-type rig. The 'bold biting' perch leaves you in no doubt that they are present and the float is decisively pulled under even by the smallest fish. They will quickly gobble down even the largest worm and the angler should strike smartly if he is to avoid a rather messy hook-extraction operation.

Minnow and spinning

Minnow and spinning are excellent ways of catching perch but may prove troublesome when pike are about. You do not require a wire trace for perch and thus the pike's teeth make short work of your nylon leader. The minnow may be fished either darted or dead baited (see page 126) but darting is by far the most effective. Live baiting was equally successful but is now illegal in Ireland.

For spinning, use either a Mepps, Toby or a small plug. Colour does not seem particularly important but an attractive darting motion is essential.

Equipment

Advising on tackle is difficult since perch may be found in all types of water, from small, heavily weeded canals to large, open, windswept lakes. Your tackle should be adapted to suit both the size of water being fished and the weight of the terminal rig.

For example, in the mid-fifties it was found that large perch were to be had in Arlesey Lake in the south of England. The fish, however, were holding in 12m of water, at a distance of 70m from the shore. To overcome the lack of boats on the lake the Arlesey bomb was developed which allowed anglers to fish a running leger at great distance. Using this technique, over seventy perch from 3 to 4¾lb (1.5-2kg) were taken in three seasons at Arlesey.

During calm weather in the months of July and August, large shoals of quite large perch (1-1¼lb; 0.5kg) appear in the midland lakes. These congregations feed avidly on perch fry and actively chase and harass their quarry about the lake; often breaking the surface during a mad, frenzied attack. Fishing from a drifting boat, perch may be taken using small mottled Mepps (sizes 0 or 1) or Toby (¼oz;12g). Another effective method of catching these shoaling perch is with a fly. Long-tailed fry imitations are best — the Hanningfield lure, Matukas, Missionary and Appetiser are ideal. The 'flies' may be fished on conventional fly tackle on a floating line, or the angler may 'jig' with them on a spinning rod.

Jigging is done by setting up one or two droppers above an Arlesey bomb. The rig can be either lowered over the side of the boat or cast towards feeding perch shoals. The jig is retrieved with a jerky sideways movement. The odd perch fry-feeding trout also falls to this method.

Handling perch

You should handle perch with the greatest of care for their spiny dorsal and opercular fins can cause quite nasty little wounds. To remove a hook, hold the fish very firmly across the back, between forefinger and thumb, immediately behind the operculars, and fold back the dorsal fin with the palm of your hand. Perch may cause problems in keepnets, both to themselves and other fish. Unless you are match fishing, you should return to the water all fish caught, or alternatively use a second keepnet.

Pike

In recent years, a new and potentially disastrous disease has struck many households in Ireland. Described by Buller, in his book *Pike* (1971), as *Esoxiparaphobia-lucius-tremens*, it is also known by the more common name of 'pike fever' and it gravely threatens the social stability of many families. Men have been known to abandon wife, children and friends for weeks on end to search for that elusive twenty- or thirty-pounder.

This dramatic change in Irish anglers' attitudes towards pike has been brought about by a recent realisation of the sporting qualities of the fish and the urgent need to conserve and manage stocks of larger pike. The formation of the Irish Pike Anglers' Club in the 1970s gave a collective voice to the views of the pike specialists and this has greatly assisted in the introduction of new conservation by-laws. There is now a national daily bag limit of three pike in all waters and an overall possession limit of ten pike. In addition, anglers may have in their possession one specimen pike on any given day. The minimum specimen weight for river pike currently stands at 20lb (9kg) and for lake pike at 30lb (13.5kg).

The boy moved slowly down the canal-like River Inny towards the legendary Lough Kinale. Casting his new 3in (7.5cm) Voblex spinner into every likely nook and cranny, he pondered on the many stories he had read regarding the voracious feeding habits and almost insane tenacity of the pike, the fish of his dreams. Pike fishing offered him the chance to catch a fish many times bigger than anything he had encountered so far in his short angling career. He knew his dad was close at hand with the newly fashioned gaff strung across his shoulders and that offered him some small consolation. Still, he was anxious and just a little nervous. What if he hooked a mad, savage ten-pounder? How could he possibly land him without sustaining some form of serious injury from those savage rows of teeth?

He worked his way slowly towards the lake. Near the confluence, the banks were marshy and soggy and a thick growth of marginal rushes and reeds prevented further progress. He moved diagonally towards the lake shore and was relieved to find a well-worn path which led him to a firm, rocky shoreline. Bordering this clear 50m stretch were dense beds of reeds, a likely spot by all accounts for a hungry pike. He waded into the water as far as his short knee-high boots would permit and cast his Voblex towards the line of rushes which garlanded the Inny mouth. He spun quickly, for he feared for his new spinner in such a weedy hostile environment.

With about ten yards to go there was a ferocious splash and his short, light rod buckled — his first pike. The fish ran towards the open lake, taking line from the carefully set slipping clutch. Confidence surged through him and images of gently beaching the monster, unaided, filled his mind. He played the fish for at least a full minute before things started to go wrong. Suddenly, for some inexplicable reason, the slipping clutch jammed. The fish was only five metres from him and he could see its olive

His first pike. The author's son David proudly displays his hard-sought prize

green back and large dorsal fin quite clearly. He inadvertently lifted the rod in his attempts to free the reel. The pike reacted violently and without so much as a by-your-leave, he vaulted out of the water and began to tailwalk to and fro in front of the small boy. The five-pound pike shook his head viciously from side to side, causing the spoon on the Voblex to rattle incessantly.

This was all too much for the boy, his young monster-ridden imagination flew in all directions at once and, turning towards the shore, he shouted for his father to save him. At the same moment the pike, following the line of least resistance, bolted towards the boy. The boy stumbled on the algae-coated rocks and pitching forward, made every effort to save his precious rod and reel from serious damage. As he struggled to his feet he felt awkward and constrained, for the ten-pound main line was tangled about his shins. Half shuffling, he made for the shore, dragging his thrashing, confused prize behind him. Screaming now in utter terror of his life, the ten-year-old glanced behind him at the flared, gaping jaws and the sunken, beady eyes.

At this point, his perplexed and concerned father arrived, gaff in hand. The sodden child scrambled towards him, in the process breaking the main line. Burying his head deep in his father's chest, he screamed, 'Oh, gaff him, gaff him, gaff him'. There was really little point for both pike and boy were now a good 10m from the water!

That first bizarre encounter with *Esox lucius* happened almost thirty seasons ago, but every frame of the event is etched in slow motion on my memory. So it is with all pike fishing: a sport packed with excitement, trepidation, satisfaction, all the basic ingredients which adorn the angler's dreams.

Life cycle and biology

Origin

The fossil history of pike can be traced back some thirty million years into the Oligocene period, long before the appearance of man, in the time of the Hairy Mammoth and the Sabre Tooth Tiger. The most surprising fact is that *Esox lucius* differs so little from its ancient ancestor (*Esox papyraceus*). On reflection, I wonder if it is so surprising, for when nature created the piscivorous pike it produced a most extraordinarily well-designed and efficient hunter. Subsequently there must have been little need to alter such a successful design.

Pike in Irish waters

Pike are not native to Ireland but in the 400 or so years since their introduction they have really made themselves at home. The greatest pike recorded was one of 90½lb (41kg) taken by John Naughton from Lough Derg, on the River Shannon, in 1862. The fish was supposedly 5½ft (1.5m) long when captured but unfortunately no reliable authentication exists. However, the capture of John Garvin's 53lb (24kg) pike, caught on Lough Conn in July 1920, is well documented. The fish was taken on a brown and gold Devon and took some forty minutes to subdue. According to some accounts, a 10lb-plus salmon was taken from its stomach prior to it being weighed! This pike was accepted as the Irish record until 1970 when a new strict regime of registering specimens and records was introduced by the Irish Specimen Fish Committee.

Since the capture of Garvin's great fish, some one hundred pike over 30lb (13.5kg) have been recorded from Irish waters. Approximately nineteen of these fish were over 40lb (18kg) and the largest was a 48lb (22kg) pike taken from Lough Mask, County Mayo, in 1963. These fish were captured either on rod and line or by netting during the course of trout stock improvement schemes on the larger midland and western lakes. The present Irish record pike is 42lb (19kg) and the fish was caught on the River Barrow in 1964. Doubtless larger pike exist.

Piscivorous species

Pike are the only truly piscivorous species of fish to be found in fresh water in Ireland. They feed mainly on trout, salmon (adults, parr and smolts), perch, rudd, roach, adult and skimmer bream. They may be highly selective at times and were exceptionally slow to adapt to a roach diet when they first appeared in Lough Derravaragh, County Westmeath, during the mid-seventies. I gained a further insight into their selectivity when surveying a small lake in County Monaghan. Our gill nets produced two brown trout and a selection of 500 rudd ranging in size from 3 or 4oz to 1lb (80–450g); yet, even with such a low proportion of trout in the lake, the largest pike caught, a fine 15lb (6.5kg) fish, had two trout in his stomach.

Pike begin actively to feed on planktonic Cladocera as soon as the yolk sac is fully absorbed, and in richer waters invertebrate food forms an important part of their diet up to a weight of 3lb (1.5kg). However, pike may and do feed on other fish from a length of 2–2½in (5–6cm); often selecting prey which are a quarter or half their own length.

Irish pike may be opportunistic in their feeding habits. I remember sampling some 300 river pike several years ago, the adults of which were feeding exclusively on crayfish (*Potamobius pallipes*). The stomachs of fish up to 8lb (3.5kg) were crammed with these creatures and there was not an unshelled fish in sight.

I have reproduced the chart below from Fitzmaurice (1981) to show the relative importance of fish and invertebrates in the diet of pike throughout various life stages:

Food item	**< 2in [< 5cm]**	**2-5½in [5-14cm]**	**Adults**
Invertebrates	95.5%	72%	-
Brown trout	–	–	51–66%
Other fish	4.5%	28%	34–49%

Growth rates

Pike are fast-growing fish, particularly in the rich Irish limestone waters, and fish of 46lb (21kg) at eight years of age have been recorded. During my work on the River Suck, I examined scales from five pike over 30lb (13.5kg) in weight, all of which were females of eight to ten years of age. The maximum lifespan of pike is probably some fourteen or fifteen years of age. Garvin's fifty-three-pounder (24kg) was aged at fourteen or perhaps fifteen years when captured. On average, a six-year-old Irish pike would weigh 20lb (9kg) while an equivalent pike from Lake Windermere would be in its fifteenth year.

After their second year, sexual dimorphism appears, with the females growing faster than the males. Of the thousands of pike examined by fisheries staff in Ireland, few males over 10lb (4.5kg) in weight have been recorded; the largest male so far recorded was 17lb (7kg). Sexing large pike is not as simple as one might imagine and a single large, distended, white ovarian sac could easily be mistaken for a male testis. Regressive ovaries can occur in female pike and to compensate the remaining ovary often becomes unusually large.

Pike

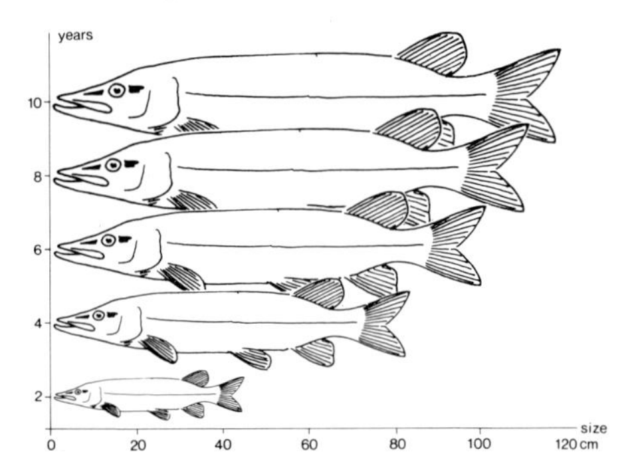

Spawning

In Irish pike, 74 per cent of the males mature in their first year, while 95 per cent of the males and 73 per cent of the females are mature at two years of age. Spawning occurs in the afternoon and a temperature of 9° to 10°C appears to be critical. The spawning season generally falls between February and April; during the earlier part of the spawning season a suitable water temperature is likely to be attained only on sunny days and then only during the afternoon and in sheltered, unshaded situations. Spawning tends to be earlier in the western lakes where temperatures rise quickly in spring.

Spawning generally takes place in shallow, sheltered situations with a bottom carpet of dead or living vegetation. Typically, the bottom is coated with various mosses, grasses or grasslike rushes

(*Agrostis* sp., *Juncus* sp. and *Fontinalis* sp.). Pike may also spawn over broken reed-mats or the flooded margins of fields. The female pike can lay upwards of 30 000 ova per kilogram of body weight and the spawn is deposited in depths of 8-24in (20-60cm) of water. While flooded lake margins may seem a rather precarious spawning site, pike ova hatch after eight to fourteen days and desiccation is rarely a problem.

Each female pike is accompanied by a host of smaller jack pike, but following spawning these must beat a hasty retreat, for the females often indulge in a feeding orgy which frequently includes their closest consorts! In the past, pike hunting at spawning time was a regular pursuit in Ireland; shotguns replaced the rod and large hen pike were stalked amongst the reeds. Annual competitions were regularly organised, particularly in the counties of Roscommon and Westmeath. So effective was the technique that the Inland Fisheries Trust adopted it in the early years of their pike removal programmes.

Quantities

Despite the rich invertebrate feeding and the plentiful supply of fodder fish, the quantity of pike flesh present in a given water is surprisingly small. It has been calculated that even in the richest waters there is little more than 35lb (16kg) of pike per hectare of water. Fodder fish may account for upwards of 220lb (100kg) per hectare. However, pike require a maintenance ration of 5:1, that is to say, they must consume 11lb (5kg) of food to maintain 1kg of their own weight. The conversion ratio in pike is approximately 7:1; thus each pike must eat 15lb (7kg) of food in addition to its maintenance ration if it is to grow by 1kg. The availability of fodder fish quickly becomes a limiting factor in pike growth.

I mentioned earlier that some one hundred pike over 30lb (13.5kg) in weight have been recorded in Ireland since 1920. Considering the effort which accompanied these captures, any would-be pike angler should be realistic in terms of his ambitions when first visiting Ireland. Fishing the best waters over a two-week period, he can realistically expect to catch several fish over 10lb (4.5kg); a twenty-pounder is always a possibility but he would need to work very hard and have the gods with him to break the elusive 30lb (13.5kg) barrier.

Behaviour

Knowing a little about pike behaviour is basic to angling success. Pike are ruthless and efficient hunters. They generally feed by day, using a combination of both eyesight and a keenly developed sense of smell or taste. For this reason they are often regarded as lone brigands and indeed Buller has gone further by declaring that they are: 'non-filial, non-territorial and non-cooperative'. The first is certainly true; any male which has survived the frantic post-spawning feeding spree of a hungry female can attest to this. The second is certainly not true but we must be careful when arguing this point to define what is meant by territory. Pike will return again and again to a native feeding zone. To my mind the fish have become accustomed to feeding in certain well-defined areas about which they may move at random. However, as Barry Rickards and Ray Webb so effectively showed in the late sixties, pike have well-defined resting lies or lairs. If the angler is fortunate enough to locate one of these sites, he can be fairly sure that at some time during the day the residents will become at least peckish. If the angler's attractively set bait is in the vicinity, he has an excellent chance of tempting the hungry pike.

When we think about it, is this behaviour really so surprising? Once it has satiated its hunger the pike returns to its 'pride' where it rests in its lair until hunger pangs recur. Because of the pike's strong cannibalistic tendencies, smaller pike are unsafe in the vicinity of such lairs. From time to time I have located concentrations of pike in confined areas and I have often noted the apparent similarity in size. The groups were either 4–8lb (2–3.5kg), 10–20lb (4.5–9kg), or apparent loners of 20lb (9kg) and above. The latter group probably consist of no more than two or three individuals. In one survey net on the River Suck I captured and released ten pike between 12 and 15lb (5.5–7kg).

Whether or not pike are co-operative feeders, I would suggest, is open to debate. Certainly, they are not co-operative feeders in the same way as perch, but they do at times gather in packs around an actively feeding shoal of fodder fish or a full keepnet. When pike surround a shoal, the very presence of several pike will disorientate the fodder fish and cause them to dart in all directions from the shoal; this leaves them wide open to attack. Pike will also gather in large numbers where shoals of fodder fish move through on a seasonal basis. This is clearly seen each April and May in Lough Corrib when pike gather in the narrows between the lake and its outflow as large concentrations of salmon smolts are migrating downstream. The pike could therefore be regarded as a facultative co-operative feeder, since the very presence of other pike improves their collective feeding success, even though they may not be conscious of a co-operative feeding venture.

Favourable water conditions

Pike feed most actively during the warmer summer months; their need for food declines in line with decreasing water temperatures and the periodicity of their feeding becomes more apparent. Pike will often adopt a very set regime of feeding times which will continue for as much as four to six weeks. A sudden change in temperature or water levels may result in a change of pattern. As a general rule, summer piking is at its best from dawn until around midday while winter pike often take best between 11.00 am and 2.00 pm. Dusk always brings the chance of pike, regardless of the time of year, and a rising barometer is also generally a good omen. When visiting a new location, a few dawn to dusk sessions will soon sort out the pike's feeding pattern for you — provided the weather remains stable. A group of companions fishing in relays can ensure that not too much sleep is lost.

It is sometimes assumed that larger pike are exclusively denizens of slow, deep water. This is often not the case and large pike are fond of such locations as warm water outflows from power stations, deeper gullies near stream/river confluences and deeper productive glides. Situated in such locations, feeding pike can easily ambush their prey which generally abound in the shallower water. To find 20 to 30lb pike (9-13.5kg) sitting in 2-2.5m of water is not such a rare occurrence.

Seasonal movements

When discussing the seasonal movements of pike in Irish waters, we should differentiate between large lakes (> 1000 acres; 400ha), smaller lakes (50-1000 acres; 20-400ha) and rivers.

The large lakes are principally spring, summer and early autumn fisheries, where little success is achieved by anglers during the depths of winter. It was originally assumed that pike hibernated during the winter period and were largely inactive. While their rate of activity may lessen with decreasing water temperatures, we have no reason to believe that they cease to feed altogether and that a mild or settled spell will not bring on renewed activity.

But where are these pike located? In the late seventies, the Central Fisheries Board commenced winter trawling operations on the larger Irish trout lakes in an effort to reduce the perch populations. It was found that both perch and other coarse fish (except roach) move into the deeper water during periods of cold weather. Here they remain practically moribund at depths of 25-30m or more until a mild spell causes the shoals to disperse. Such shoals re-form as soon as the water temperatures drop sufficiently. Surrounding the fodder fish are concentrations of feeding pike.

The arrival of roach in many of the larger lakes is certainly making a difference to pike behaviour and consistently good shore pike fishing has been reported from the Crookedwood end of Lough Derravaragh during the past two or three seasons (1986-89). Several pike over 20lb (9kg) have been recorded, and one monster, with an estimated weight of 40lb+ (18kg), was returned alive in January 1989. A similar pattern will almost certainly develop in other roach-infested waters.

In the smaller lakes and rivers winter pike are more accessible and these fisheries may continue to perform well throughout the winter period. In river fisheries, winter piking is at its best under settled water conditions, regardless of the temperature; pike are to be found in the deeper, slow-flowing areas during this time.

Angling for pike is quite different to any other form of coarse angling; pike are heavier, the tackle used is stronger and several unique items of tackle are required. The true specialist pike angler will possess a great array of tackle, including thermometers, barometers and gargantuan keepnets. However, I propose to deal only with what I consider essential items of tackle.

Rods

Pike rods vary from standard 6 to 8ft (2–3m) spinning rods to specially designed 10 to 11ft (3–3.5m) fast, tapered, hollow fibreglass or carbon rods with a test curve of 2 to 2½lb (1kg). Such rods are used for long-distance legering. Rods with a softer action and a more gentle taper are used with soft baits, such as rudd and roach. It is not essential that pike rods display a definite pedigree but the rod should match the requirements. Dead bait fishing with a short light spinning rod may not alone be frustrating, it may also prove dangerous. Last season I was caught unawares when several fine pike invaded a rudd swim which I was fishing. A hasty and clumsy effort to hand-throw a 5oz (140g) dead rudd towards the feeding pike resulted in a size 6 treble hook becoming embedded deep in my index finger.

Reels/Line

I would suggest a fixed-spool reel for all spinning and dead baiting. A multiplier has a lot to offer when trolling, both in terms of immediate contact with the fish and the sensitivity of the drag-and-ratchet settings. Reels should be fully loaded with at least 200m of 10–15lb (4.5–6.5kg) nylon. A short, 6–10m section of heavier nylon, or shock leader, may be required for really long-distance dead baiting. In such circumstances a light beachcaster may also be used.

Floats

A range of pike bungs are readily available but a common mistake is to choose a float which is too big and too buoyant. As a general rule, choose a float between one and two inches (2.5–5cm) in diameter. Pike floats are easily manufactured and you may fashion your own designs quite easily from a series of bottle corks, some Superglue and a sheet of smooth sandpaper. Cigar-shaped floats and a dumb-bell design are becoming increasingly popular in Ireland. The dumb-bell float is simply two 1in (2.5cm) cork pilot floats joined by a hollow peg. The line is passed through the centre of the float and the hollow peg is plugged. The float is more sensitive than the standard bung design and may also be used as a slider.

Wire

When pike fishing, always use a wire trace. A 12–14in (30–35cm) trace is generally sufficient except when fishing a static dead bait, when an 18in (46cm) trace is often required. Braided, multistrand wire is the most dependable but single-strand wire may be used for dead baiting — Alasticum is a good brand. If the wire becomes kinked, throw it away. To connect wire to a swivel, hook or bait, simply pass some 4in (10cm) or so of wire, twice, through its eye and holding it steady, twist the wire into neat folds; cut off the sharp ends and if you wish to be really certain of the knot holding, apply a drop of Superglue. Commercial wire traces for spinning have a swivel attached to one end and a quick-release snap attachment at the other end. The patent attachment makes changing baits quick and simple, but be careful, for some of these may prise open with prolonged casting or snap open in a large fish. If there is a chance of a 10lb+ pike, connect the spinning bait directly to the wire as described above.

Gags
Removing hooks from deep in a pike's throat can be a dangerous business both for the pike and the angler. For this reason pike gags were invented. These are strongly sprung U-shaped pieces of metal which are inserted into the pike's mouth. Once the safety clip is released, the gag springs open and ensures that the pike cannot close his jaws. The commercial variety are sold, for some unknown reason, with sharp U-shaped points on either arm of the gag. If used as bought, this type of gag will damage the roof or floor of the pike's mouth. File down the points and build up the extremities of each arm using insulating tape.

Bite indicators
A whole range of battery-operated bite indicators are now available. The basic principle is that of a broken circuit which is completed once a fish snatches the line from the groove in the indicator. An alarm sounds and the angler is put on notice that the fish has taken the bait; a fast strike ensures against gut-hooking and irreparable damage to the pike. Bite indicators are most useful at dawn and dusk when light is at a minimum. They are also useful when more than one rod is in use.

Dead baiting

As mentioned previously, live baiting is now banned in Ireland. However well-intentioned and desirable this move, it is certainly a handicap which serious pike anglers could well do without. However, we must abide by the law of the land and we are therefore left with two principal methods of catching pike, dead baiting and the use of artificials. Dead baiting may be further subdivided into legering, float legering and wobbled dead bait.

Bait

The normal dead baits used by Irish anglers include roach, rudd, skimmer bream, herrings and mackerel; proprietary baits such as smelt, sprats and sardines are now more freely available and have proven exceptionally effective. In general the size of a dead bait varies between 2 and 6oz (60–180g) and rarely is a bait over 8oz (230g) used. It has often been said that larger pike follow a 10 per cent rule; that is to say, the preferred size of their prey approximates to 10 per cent of their own body weight. While this may be true, a pike would find it difficult to thrive in many waters if he adhered rigidly to his preferences, for the bulk of the fodder fish in most waters are less than ¾lb (340g). I am convinced that even the largest pike could be tempted by an attractively presented 6oz (170g) natural bait.

Half herring or mackerel may also be used as a dead bait and these are becoming increasingly popular for winter pike fishing. The tail-half of the fish is generally used, although the portion containing the head is equally effective. By cutting the bait in half, the angler releases the attractive and pungent fish oils which draw marauding pike.

Many anglers have found that although herring and mackerel may prove highly successful initially, on a given water, their effectiveness declines over time. It is not clear whether this is due to an element of learning on the part of the pike, but, whatever the reason, it would seem that these baits should be used selectively. Of the two, mackerel is often given credit for its extra firm musculature and extreme oiliness.

Legering

Leger rigs consist of an 18in (45cm) two-hook Jardine snap tackle connected by a swivel to the main line. A free-running Arlesey bomb may be slipped unto the main line above the swivel, if required, but normally the dead bait's own weight is sufficient for casting. Where a bomb is used, a leger stop, placed some 2-3m along the main line, completes the rig.

The fish is mounted onto the snap tackle by inserting the single hook into the backbone of the fish just above the tail. The treble hook is placed in the fish just behind the dorsal fin. Hooks should not be too large, sizes 8 to 10 for the treble and sizes 6 to 8 for the single. If fish continuously lift the bait without the runs developing, the single hook should be removed and the remaining treble inserted in its place. If you prefer you may first insert the wire through the flesh of the fish using a long sacking needle and insert the treble through the backbone between the dorsal fin and the tail.

Pike have exceptionally hard bony mouths and you should ensure that your hook points are needle sharp at all times. When using freshwater fish remember to burst their swim-bladder before use. This is done by inserting a long needle two or three times vertically through their back and into the body cavity. The swim-bladder causes the bait to float; this may be used to your advantage in a situation where the bed of the lake is coated in a thick mass of weeds. Simply slip on a small leger above the swivel and leave the fish's swim-bladder intact. The bomb will ensure that the rig sinks but the buoyant fish will rise just above the weed layer.

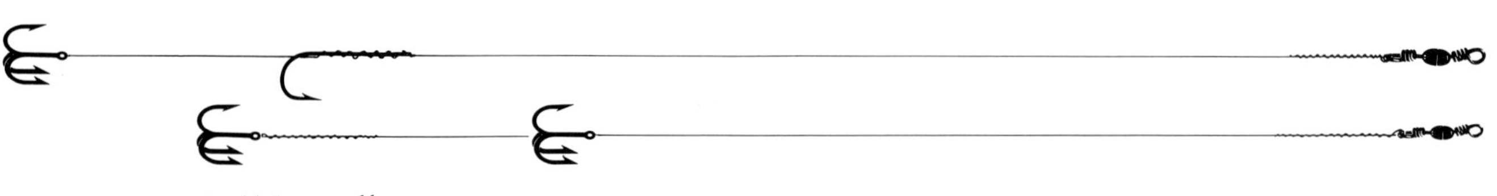

Dead bait snap tackles

Float legering

Suspended dead baits, as their name implies, are fished on a float rig and they are normally fished either on, or just above, the bottom. A slider float is used with a swan-shot located some 6in (15cm) above the swivel and a bead just above the float. A stop-knot is placed at an appropriate point along the main line and the bead prevents the leger-stop running through the aperture of the bung float. The float is set to float on, or just below, the water's surface. Pike may, at times, be quite fastidious regarding the actual location of the dead bait. The angler should not fish blindly for many hours with the bait located in the one position, but rather should alter its position in the water column from time to time. When attacking a dead bait, pike seem all too well aware that the fish is lifeless, so there is no need to worry about the positioning of the bait. The fish is not concerned whether it is vertical or horizontal, hooked by the tail, back or head.

Traditionally, when legering a dead bait you were advised to wait for the second run before striking; for the fish normally takes the bait across his jaws, runs for a short distance, falters while he repositions the bait in his mouth, so that it may be swallowed head first, and then takes a second longer run. In the interests of conservation it is now recommended that the angler strike on the first run. This will result in a lip-hooked fish, which can be returned to the water in tip-top condition. Some additional pike may be lost but the use of small hooks and dead baits should result in the pike fully engulfing the bait before moving off on his first run.

Wobbled dead baiting

The final method of using a dead bait is my own firm favourite and may be described as the wobbled dead bait. A snap tackle with two treble-hooks is used; one is inserted through the lower lip and roof of the bait's mouth, the second is placed in the flank of the fish, just behind the dorsal fin. The distance between the two trebles is such that the fish must be bent to insert the second treble. The wire trace is normally bound to the flank of the fish using strong, but very fine, elastic thread. A barrel or wye lead is inserted onto the main line above the 18–24in (45–60cm) trace. This is held in place by either a leger-stop or a second swivel.

The bait is fished close to the bottom and the rate of retrieve is varied until it attracts a pike; the bait should wobble and dart like an injured fish, but it should not spin. On some days, particularly when water temperatures are higher, the pike may prefer a faster-moving bait. I prefer freshwater fish for this method as I have found that both herring and mackerel are prone to pulling loose from the snap tackle.

A wobbled dead bait may be successfully fished at all times of the year and it is particularly attractive to marauding or hunting pike. Pike take the bait in much the same way as a trout or perch takes a minnow; they swim past the bait and turn, taking it head first. The fish are generally hooked high in the mouth and more often than not one of the hooks is dangling free. Where a fish swirls at the bait but does not take it, the angler should increase the speed of the retrieve, and when the pike has swirled at the bait, let it sink to the bottom. The pike will either take it on the drop or return after a short while and pick up the bait from the bottom.

Artificials

Pike are taken on a wide range of artificial lures, including plugs, spinners and a huge variety of spoon baits. Artificials are most useful during the warmer summer months when the pike are at their most active. They are also in the peak of condition and will frequently treat the angler to acrobatic jumps and vivid displays of 'tail walking'.

Plugs

Plugs may be roughly divided into two groups: floaters and sinkers. Some of the more modern plugs have a frontal metal vane, the position of which may be altered to permit the plug to fish shallow or deep. Plugs may be further subdivided into jointed or unjointed. For summer piking under calm, warm conditions, a floating jointed plug is best.

When you see some evidence of pike activity (swirls or splashes on the surface of the water or small rudd or roach jumping clear of the water), cast your plug over the area and let it settle. Give the reel two or three fast turns and let the plug re-surface, then repeat the procedure. Remember that the faster you retrieve the plug, the deeper it will dive. Pike will often take the plug just after it starts to move or as it floats to the surface. The take is savage and is accompanied by a great splash on the surface and the gnashing of interlocking rows of teeth and the snapping of powerful jaws.

When the wind is blowing hard you may usefully substitute an unjointed, slow-sinking plug. The bait need not be too large, 2-4in (5-10cm) is generally sufficient. Colour is often important; pike seem to prefer natural ranges rather than the great gaudy concoctions which some tackle manufacturers would have us believe are 'real killers'. Amongst my own favourite pike colours are red, green and black, often accompanied by a flash of yellow. Pike can be choosy at times and it pays to experiment.

Spoons and spinners

In Ireland, the traditional pike spoon is a plain copper and silver in sizes ranging from 2 to 5in (5-13cm). It is still a very effective bait, especially when trolled. In addition, there are now a whole range of baits available including kidney shapes, bar shapes and even seductive fish shapes. The Toby, in either copper and silver, copper and gold or black and gold is also an ideal pike bait.

I have one plain 3in (7.5cm) red and white striped spoon which is now battered and torn from pikes' teeth but continues to catch fish. A smaller 2in (5cm) version which I purchased on the same day has not, as yet, caught me a single fish. I have had a similar experience with salmon spinners and this has led me to the conclusion that the angler should treasure a successful artificial, for there is no guarantee that an exact replacement will have that hidden extra which attracts fish after fish.

Colour is also important in spoons and spinners and again choose a fairly natural basic colour. In cold water, fish the baits slow and deep and give the pike plenty of opportunity to see them.

Trolling

Deepwater trolling for pike in the great Irish lakes is more akin to sea angling than any other branch of the sport. Lough Corrib, for example, has a surface area of 44 000 acres (18 000ha); Lough Allen, County Leitrim, is in comparison a mere pond but still covers an acreage of 8700 acres (3500ha); and the limestone-rich midland lakes range in size from 2500 acres (1000ha) to well over 4000 acres (1600ha).

These inland seas are relatively shallow, but they may contain some surprisingly deep trenches reaching down to 30m or more. The bottom may also be strewn with massive limestone boulders, much larger than the average two-storey house. The perimeter of these boulder formations may shelve into 9m of water. In contrast, there are vast, shallow, productive bays between 2 and 3m in depth, surrounded by thick bands of reeds and rushes and containing an unbelievably rich fauna and flora.

The pike angler must therefore seek out his quarry in the most confusing and heterogeneous of habitats. Traditionally, pike are taken on these lakes by trolling large 3-5in (8-13cm) plain copper and silver spoons through known taking areas; shallow water (less than 4.5m) is scorned and the baits are normally fished on a long line (50 to 80m) without the addition of extra lead. It is assumed that the length of the line and the weight of the spinner will guarantee sufficient depth. The method does work and has in the past taken some extraordinary bags of pike.

Locating taking areas

The principal limitation on the visiting angler is the location of the potential taking areas. Even with the most willing local assistance, the location of a lake hotspot, which may encompass no more than 1000m^2, in a vast unfamiliar lake is difficult if not impossible. To delineate the contours of the lake bed and to construct a three-dimensional image of the lake bottom, a small mobile echo-sounder is an almost indispensable piece of modern equipment. There are depth charts available for several of the larger lakes but even where such charts do exist, an echo-sounder is required to pinpoint the angler's location vis-à-vis some of the more attractive underwater features. The transducer, which emits and receives the signal from the sounder, may be sited either fore or aft. It is better, if at all possible, to keep it well removed from the disturbance caused by the engine.

In deepwater trolling the angler should search out shelves, trenches and gullies. Summer pike may be found in depths of 9m or more, for in these clearwater lakes swards of rich vegetation attract fodder fish to these depths and beyond. Before each transect of the lake the serious troller notes his position by taking marks and in this way he can, if successful, return to his starting point. Using a chart recorder, a crude contour map may be constructed by retaining the records of all longitudinal and transverse transects. The location of each transect is drawn on a blank map of the lake and the various depth points are recorded. By joining corresponding depth locations, a contour map gradually takes shape. The depth map of Lough Allen, County Longford, shown in the illustration, was constructed in this manner over a two-day period. It is certainly not an Admiralty chart but is more than sufficient to guarantee successful angling.

Using a downrigger

Defining the depth contours is only one of the obstacles which the troller must overcome. He must also ensure that his bait is fishing at the appropriate depth. This is where the downrigger comes into its own. Originally these were manufactured from the butts of old sea rods and a centrepin reel containing 50 to 100m of strong braided nylon. Attached to the braided line was a 2 to 4lb (1–2kg) lead weight. This line was marked off in yards or metres and the lead was lowered to the required fishing depth. The fishing line was first attached near the lead using either a strand of cotton or light nylon. When a fish took, the connector broke and the angler was in direct contact with his fish.

Fiddling about with thread connectors as the boat moved along was a messy business and several new patent downriggers, incorporating a quick release mechanism, are now available. One of the best of these is the Tidebeater, which also incorporates a hand-brake and a depth recorder.

Deep trolling should be carried out over a range of depths and it pays to experiment with both the size and variety of baits used; plain spoons, bar spoons, plugs and even spun deadbaits are all worth a try. Pike are not the only predatory fish to inhabit the depths; ferox trout, salmon, sea trout and even large perch are also taken by the deepwater troller.

Care of the fish

Pike have now gained the status of true sport fish and are generally afforded the care and consideration which they deserve. However, in some angling quarters pike are still regarded as a type of vermin and little thought is given either to their landing or to the post-capture procedures which are so

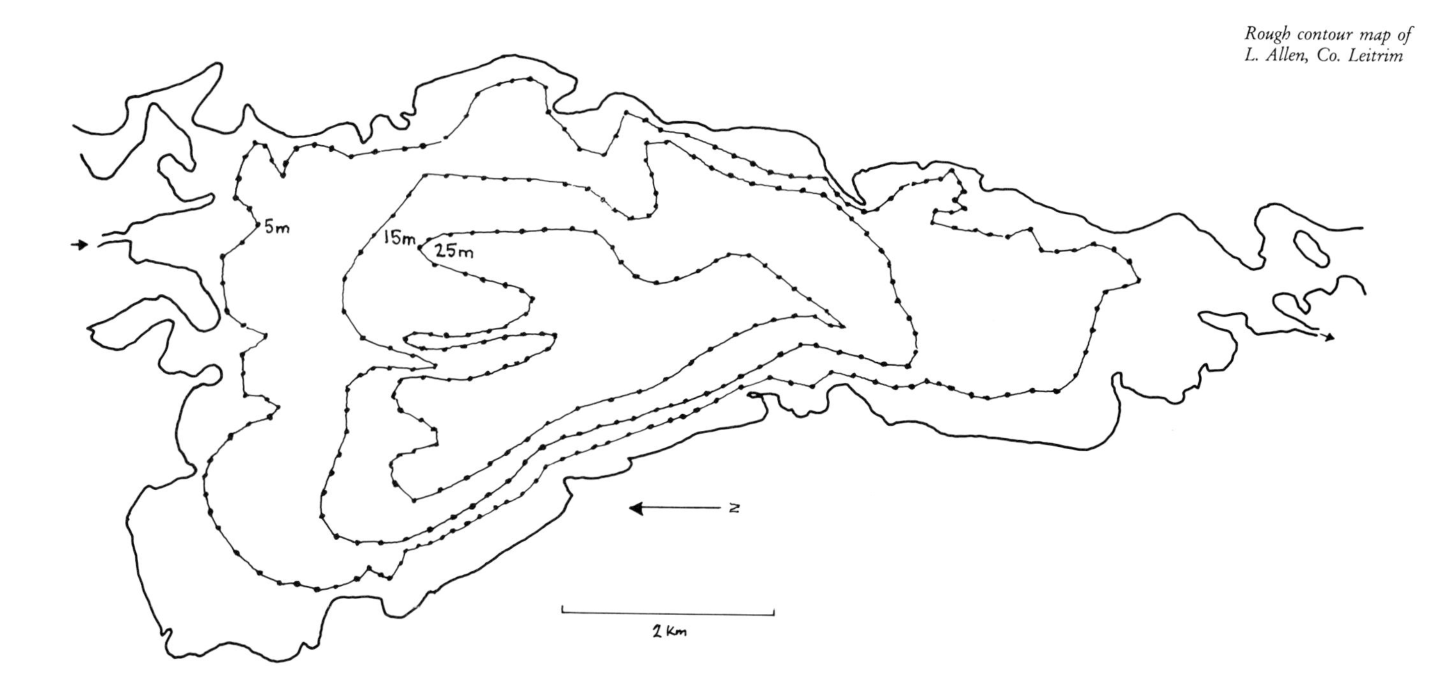

Rough contour map of L. Allen, Co. Leitrim

important in returning a lively and healthy fish to its environment.

Pike have very distinctive markings and pike specialists often photograph the mottled patterns of the larger fish. Using such distinguishing features they can identify individuals. In recent years it is known that some large pike have appeared at least twice on the annual specimen lists of the Irish Specimen Fish Committee.

The recapture of these large pike also emphasises the relative scarcity of such fine specimens in any one water and reinforces the view that really large pike can quickly disappear from a fishery if reasonable conservation measures are not adhered to.

Gaffs

Gaffs are an abomination and I have grown to hate them with a vengeance. They are a danger, not alone to the fish but also to the careless angler. Many years ago I slipped while spinning for bass near Monatrea House, Youghal, and impaled my forearm on the point of a homemade gaff.

Following the pain, distress and inconvenience of that episode, I all but abandoned the use of a gaff in fresh water.

Nets

Most modern pike anglers use large triangular or circular nets when fishing for 15lb+ fish and a diameter of 24 to 36in (60-90cm) is required. The one disadvantage of a net is that a companion is required to use it effectively. Pike up to 10lb (4.5kg) may be readily netted by the lone angler but landing anything bigger before it is totally exhausted is definitely a two-man job. A long, light but strong handle is very useful; avoid the standard hollow fibreglass handles used in coarse angling nets for they will buckle under the weight of any decent pike. Loose hooks may also foul the netting, but if the pike has been folded into the net when landed this is not a major problem. Do not waste time in attempting to free the hook, simply nip the wire trace if a free hook is caught, or cut the offending stem of the treble along the shank or at the bend.

Removing hooks

If you have netted a large pike, (10lb or more), tip him gently out onto a plastic sack. Cover his body with the sack and roll him over onto his back. Straddle the pike and with gloved hands (strong gardening gloves are ideal), pull the lower jaw towards you. Holding the trace taut, locate the hook and, if the fish is hooked deep in the throat, insert a blunt, taped gag. Using an artery forceps or a long-nosed pliers, push back against the hook to release it. If the pike is small, leave him in the net and, holding him firmly about the back of his neck, remove the hook as described.

Some authors recommend inserting an artery forceps into the gills of the fish in order to retrieve hooks. I have grave reservations regarding this: it is equivalent to poking about with a great ignorant lump of metal in the delicate tissue of a human lung. The fine gill filaments are easily damaged and the accompanying haemorrhage can result in the pike bleeding to death; particularly if he makes for deep water when released. If a pike's gills are badly damaged either by the angler's hooks or by efforts to retrieve them, I would strongly advise that the pike be quickly and humanely killed rather than being released to a slow and painful death.

Weighing pike

The strong coating of slime on the pike's body and its scales constitute a critical anti-infection barrier. If a portion of this protection is lost the pike is left open to infection by a whole range of fungi, bacteria and water-borne parasites. When weighing pike, never poke the scales under the gill cover, rather place the fish in a sack or sling.

PIKE TROLLING TECHNIQUES

Lough Ree is probably one of the finest mixed fisheries remaining in Europe. Its 26 000 acres (10 500ha) of water contain vast shoals of every coarse fish species (except dace) available in Ireland today, migrating salmon in season and some of the most challenging natural trout fishing in Ireland. Outside of Ireland it is principally famous as a pike fishery but in recent years it has gained an unsurpassed reputation for large rudd/bream hybrids and for the quality of its roach, particularly where the river Inny enters the lake.

But this afternoon is to be dedicated to the pursuit of large Lough Ree pike, a pastime dear to my companion's heart and one in which he has invested a great deal of time and effort. The wind is a good force 6 and a little gusty, which Paul reckons are ideal conditions; but I am a little nervous at venturing out in our small boat. We both struggle into our life jackets and the solid, buoyant feel of its material gives me some small reassurance.

We are going deep trolling and Paul's small, 14ft (4m), boat is well adapted for this purpose. Near the stern, on the port side, he has clamped on a downrigger; it is a Tidebeater (see page 227). Near the prow of the boat is a second clamp which holds the transducer belonging to a small, portable echo-sounder. Two trolling mounts, for the rods, are also clamped along the port side. Paul's trolling rod is a strong 8ft (2.5m) hollowglass rod with a top-quality winch fitting. Onto this is placed a Daiwa multiplier holding 250m of 15lb (6.5kg) nylon. An anti-kink swivel and 18in (45cm) multi-strand wire trace are attached to the main line. Paul chooses a large 2oz (56g) black and gold Toby to start.

I should mention here that Lough Ree, like so many of our great Irish lakes, is a vast, shallow, windswept sheet of water which can quite quickly generate enormous waves, particularly when the winds blow directly down the long axis of the lake. Visitors should not take these lakes lightly and if at all possible should engage the services of a local gillie on their first few outings. Certainly I would advise against small light craft, such as our own, unless one is familiar with the lake and its subtle change of moods. A standard 16 or 18ft (5-6m) clinker-built wooden boat is the more usual craft to use when fishing these larger lakes.

We motor out into the wave, searching for a long shelving trench somewhere between 10 and 15m deep. Most of the lake seems to be between 3 and 4.5m but as we come close to one of the larger islands, I see the depth marker slip down towards 6, 8, 10 and finally 15m. Paul knows from experience that this gulley lies west/south west off the point of the island. It is approximately 1.5km long and a half kilometre wide and holds several pike hotspots. We move to the lee of the island and slowly motor out until we reach the start of the trench. As the boat moves along, I lower the bait over the side, connect it to the quick-release clip and release the brake to allow the 4lb (2kg) weight down to 3 or 4m. Keeping close to the bank of the trench, we motor along at a moderately slow pace.

Within seconds, the multiplier screeches. I anxiously grab the rod and strike. Paul laughs, for experience has taught him that this often happens at the start of a run. The bait had snagged in some dense stonewort as we moved off the shelf at the back of the island. I retrieve the spinner, clear the few remaining strands of algae from it and re-attach it to the downrigger.

As we troll, Paul explains that really large pike are not always found at great depths and that in general they seem to favour deeper water between feeding forays. In much the same way as river pike hold in specific lairs, lake pike also have their favourite lies. These are generally to be found in the deeper water off shelves and gullies. As the pike become peckish they move from the shelf into the shallower water in search of food. Because of the distances which are covered when trolling, you stand an excellent chance of locating a larger pike in or near a deep trench. Large pike can be taken in shallow water but you would need to know certain areas of the lake exceptionally well before you could predict their feeding patterns and movements. When they are concentrated in resting packs, one is far more likely to encounter a good fish.

Just as I notice that the depth readings are beginning to even off, the taut point of the rod springs free as the line is jerked from the patent clip, 4m or so under the surface. The ratchet on the multiplier screams and Paul cuts the engine. I lift the rod free of its mount and feel the characteristic darting movements of a lively 6lb (2.5kg) pike. The boat slows and the fish is quickly under control. It is lip-hooked and released unharmed back into the lake.

We decide to re-fish the trench but without success. By this time the wind is really quite strong and even Paul admits that we should make our way back towards Inny Bay. He suggests that we venture out into the main lake where a deep 20–25m trench stretches northwards towards our home bay.

Without too much difficulty we locate the trench, but I then realise that we must motor across the waves if we are to follow its contour! We set a large 5in (13cm) copper and silver spoon at 8m and move along from trough to peak, dipping and bobbing amongst the choppy waves. At times, the engine whines and the boat tilts at a most disconcerting angle, but Paul's experience gently eases us along.

I am holding on firmly to the gunwales of the boat but with a weather eye to the depth gauge. As Paul predicted, the trench is on average some 20m deep but at times it rises quite steeply to 10m or slightly less. Some seconds after we have passed over one of these sub-surface peaks, the spoon is grabbed 8m below us by a large set of powerful jaws! The line snaps free and the rod tip almost breaks in two with the rock-solid resistance offered by the great fish. Was it my imagination or did the motion of the boat even falter?

Paul cuts the engine, I stand, lift the rod and to my surprise I feel nothing except a dead heavy weight. Am I stuck fast in the bottom? As the boat slows and begins to drift eastwards with the waves, the pike seems to realise that he is hooked and that his best chance of escape is at the surface. I can actually feel the great body, rising, rising in the water. I gain line as he moves. Suddenly and quite unexpectedly the mighty fish breaks the surface some 30m from the boat and churns the waves into foam as he aggressively crashes his head from side to side, seeking to rid himself of the persistent steel. Frustrated at his lack of success, the fish makes straight for the boat and half arches out of the water with only 5m to go. He dives under the boat and almost pulls me off balance as he plunges deep below us. Paul is on the oars and he expertly brings the boat around over the main line as I fight the fish out of the stern of the boat. The fish continues his run and Paul brings the boat around in a full circle so that I am once again fishing off the port side. The pike makes several more deep runs but each time I can sense that his energy is sapping. He avoids any further surface activity and we do not see him again until he rolls lethargically in the waves near to the boat. Paul's great net reaches out into the water and my prize is hauled aboard. He looks to be well in excess of 20lb (9kg) but Paul assures me that he is nearer 15lb (7kg). The scales shows him to be 16lb 6oz (7.5kg); a fine pike nonetheless.

Paul re-starts the engine as I remove the spinner from the pike's throat. I roll him over on his back and with my hands protected by strong gardening gloves, I pull his lower jaw towards me. A strong pair of artery forceps quickly removes the two hooks of the treble which are buried deep in the pike's oesophagus. It is a beautiful deep, short bodied pike, light olive green in colour and obviously in the peak of condition. With a gentle and admiring pat on the side, I slip my prize over the gunwales.

By this time a full storm is raging. We decide to call it a day and to make for the lee of some neighbouring islands from which we can quickly steam towards the safety of Inny Bay.

The popular downrigger manufactured by Tidebeater Ltd.

CHAPTER 6

EELS & CARP

Fishing for eels and carp may not seem to have a great deal in common but it is rumoured that serious eel fishing first started when bored English carp anglers adopted it as a means of occupying the long hours between carp bites. As carp became educated to various techniques and more and more difficult to catch, anglers found that long days rather than hours of serious effort were required to deceive their primary quarry. By snatching out a few small rudd or roach from the margins of the carp pond, they provided themselves with sufficient bait to last several hours. Eventually this secondary pursuit became the primary passion and this in turn led to the formation of the National Anguilla Club.

Eel and carp fishing are definitely minority sports in Ireland but both species grow to quite large proportions and are well worth more serious consideration by anglers.

Eels

Life cycle and biology

Catadromous life cycle

The life cycle of the eel is even more interesting and more extraordinary than that of the salmon. There are two very closely related species: the American eel (*Anguilla rostrata*) and the European eel (*Anguilla anguilla*). The young migrate from the sea into fresh water to feed and the resultant adults migrate back to the sea to reproduce; this form of life cycle is known to biologists as 'catadromous'.

Spawning

Adult eels spawn collectively during March and April in the Sargasso Sea (23°-26°N/69°-74°W) at a depth of 100 to 300m. The Sargasso Sea is an area of ocean lying in the south-west corner of the Atlantic Ocean surrounding the island of Bermuda. It contains some extraordinarily deep trenches and the ocean bed lies at 6000m in places. European eels thus spawn at a distance of between 4000 and 8000 kilometres from their native rivers in Europe and North Africa.

One of the most unusual features of the eel is that the sex of each individual is determined after hatching; both genotype and environmental factors are known to play a part in regulating sexual dominance.

After hatching, the pelagic larvae of the eel are known as *leptocephali* and flattened from side to side and almost transparent in appearance. The larvae are carried by prevailing ocean currents to America, North Africa and Europe. The Gulf Stream carries the larvae towards Ireland and as it does so, the *leptocephali* go through a series of changes.

After a period of three years the young eels, known now as elvers, reach our estuaries and bays. Although their time of arrival is variable, 2 to 3in (5-7.5cm) elvers normally appear in early spring along our western coastline. Their entry into fresh water is regulated more by water temperature — which must have reached 9°C — than by date.

Growth rates

Eels are relatively slow-growing and adult males will normally average from 11 to 20in (30-50cm), while females average 16.5 to 39in (40-100cm). These fish may be from eight to twenty years of age and indeed in situations where they are denied access to the sea, they may live until they are forty years old.

Feeding habits

Eels are principally nocturnal feeders but they may also be caught during the day. Amongst their principal dietary items are crustaceans, snails, insect larvae, small fish, mussels and even frogs. Contrary to their reputation as lovers of mud, the larger fish certainly seem to prefer gravel or stones. Fish remains are generally found in the stomachs of eels greater than 16in (40cm) in length and even then are not very common. Strangely, however, anglers' experience is that fish are by far the most popular form of eel bait. Perhaps eels are inept at catching fish and that is why an attractively presented dead bait works so well.

Migratory instinct

Eels have a propensity to migrate throughout their lives in fresh water but there is a gradual reduction in such mass movements as the fish grow older. In Ireland, most adult upstream migrations occur in the May-to-July period. Even after they have spent several years in one general locality, eels may resume their upstream migration. However, in the larger systems one usually finds that the middle to lower reaches are packed with eels, but that they are relatively scarce in the upper reaches.

When they have reached maturity the adult yellow eels, as they are called, change into silver eels; their eyes enlarge, the jaw muscles shrink and the head takes on a markedly pointed appearance. The eel's back turns black while the ventral surface adopts a bright silvery sheen. They cease to feed but almost one quarter of their total body weight now consists of stored fat for the journey ahead. It has been calculated that, to reach their spawning sites in the Sargasso Sea by March or

April, mature eels must travel at speeds of between twenty and forty kilometres per hour.

Eels begin their mammoth migration on cold, dark, moonless November nights when the parent rivers are swollen with winter rains. They are trapped at this point of their life cycle by commercial fisheries such as those on the River Shannon and the River Corrib. They constitute a very valuable commercial harvest. Some of the larger Irish lakes produce exceptionally high densities of eels. Lough Neagh, for example, Ireland's largest lake, produces an incredible harvest of 20kg per hectare per year, or 100 tonnes of eels.

Few eels have been captured during their southward spawning migration and it is not known how they navigate or at what level of the ocean. It is further assumed that adults die after spawning, but again this has never been verified.

Eels are exceptionally hardy fish and it is only when you have a large eel on the bank that the real contest begins! Because of their glutinous, slimy coat and narrow gill-slits they can live for very long periods out of water. They can also survive on their fat store for prolonged periods and have lived for up to four years without food.

Eel angling

Eels are affectionately known as 'snakes' or 'serpents' by many coarse anglers. They were originally excluded, along with salmonids, from coarse angling competitions; no one really seems to know why. In recent times the inclusion of eels has become more widespread and indeed in Britain 'eel only' competitions are now being organised.

The British record eel stands at an incredible 11lb 2oz (5kg), but much larger eels have been recorded from commercial fisheries. The current Irish record stands at 6lb 15oz (3kg) but an eel of 48in (120cm) and weighing 8lb (3.5kg) was recorded by Noel Hackett during a stock survey of the Lough, Cork city, in September 1974. While on holidays in Wexford in 1962, my father and I also caught a 48in (120cm) eel from the Owenavorragh River on a small dead bait. It was long before the Irish Specimen Fish Committee recognised the eel as a worthy addition to their schedule of fish. We did not weigh the eel but measured it carefully. I do not know what weight it was, but my aunt's three cats and two dogs were still being served portions of eel two days after its capture!

Whatever about record eels, there is certainly an abundance of eels in Irish waters over the present specimen weight of 3lb (1.5kg). The best locations for large eels are the limestone lakes of the central plain and the lower reaches of the larger limestone rivers. Surprisingly large eels may also be found in small rich ponds but they are probably quite old individuals which have been denied ready access to the sea.

Bait

Eels are mostly taken on large worms or smallish fish baits; minnow, rudd, roach, sprat and pilchards have all proven successful. One of the most readily accessible baits in many Irish river catchments is the minnow. Small rudd and roach are also suitable; one- and two-year-old fish are best but your bait should be no longer than about 3 or 4in (7.5–10cm).

Some anglers prefer to use fish portions or puncture the bait several times to release the attractive fish oils; puncturing also deflates the swim-bladder which will cause it to float if left intact. As is the case with pike, herring or mackerel portions might also prove attractive to eels. It is known that Irish eels will selectively feed on crustaceans and for that reason small crayfish, prawns or shrimps are also well worth a try.

To mount the bait, use a sacking needle to pass the line through the vent and out at the mouth; attach a long-shanked size 6 or 8 hook and pull the eye and shank into the fish, leaving the bend, point and barb exposed. Attach a bead or small split-shot to the line where it leaves the vent. Use a standard running leger rig to complete the tackle. At all costs avoid treble-hooks or snap tackles.

Eels are very slow to take a bait and will often attack it intermittently over several minutes, before finally consuming it. If you watch an eel in clear water you will see it lift the bait and shake its head vigorously from side to side, as if tearing at it, before dropping it and resting adjacent to the bait. This process is repeated several times until the bait is swallowed. The eel will then often rest on the bottom without indicating a trace of movement on the line.

Removing hooks

Extracting hooks from eels is a dreadful business, particularly at night. Bring with you plenty of spare ready-mounted baits and a large dry sack. Haul your eel up onto the sack, and the dry surface will subdue, to some extent, its gyrations. Put a fold of the sack over the eel's back and hold it firmly — much easier said than done. Extract the hook with a pliers or artery forceps. When night fishing it is best to nip the line and re-attach a second, ready-mounted bait. Store your eels in a keepnet.

If you intend to keep your eels for the table, a sharp blow to the side of the fish just forward of the vent, adjacent to an organ known as the lymph heart, will immobilise it while you extract the hook. It seems there is a nerve plexus located at this point which controls most of its snakelike movements. A deep nick just behind the head is the most humane way of killing eels destined for the pot.

Carp

Life cycle and biology

Introduction into Ireland

The carp (*Cyprinus carpio*) is an Asiatic species whose original distribution stretched from Manchuria in China to the rivers of the Black Sea and eastwards into Japan. Carp have been cultivated as a food fish for at least 2000 years and as a consequence their distribution has spread westwards, far beyond their native range. It is claimed that the Romans first introduced carp into western Europe and that their popularity as a food and ornamental fish reached its peak between the thirteenth and fifteenth centuries.

Introductions into Ireland prior to 1950 were both sporadic and largely abortive. Richard Boyle, the Great Earl of Cork, is reputed to have introduced carp in 1634 and 1640. There are other vague references to further introductions at later dates but such references are lacking in detail. However, we do know that the stocking of carp was largely confined to the counties of Dublin, Wexford, Cork and Tipperary. Appendix 2 gives a detailed account of the known distribution of carp in Ireland up to the present day and was compiled with the assistance of my colleague, Paddy Fitzmaurice, a well-known authority on Irish freshwater and marine fish. It is largely based on a scientific paper published by Paddy in 1983.

Genetic selection

Farmed carp were selected over the centuries for their fast growth rate and improved weight to length ratio. This has resulted in the production of deep-bodied, high-shouldered races of carp which are in direct contrast with the more streamlined natural forms.

Genetic selection has also led to the production of at least three distinct strains of carp: common carp are fully scaled but deeper than the ancestral form; mirror carp are largely devoid of scales but rows of exceptionally large scales may be present along the dorsal surface, below the dorsal fin, along the lateral line or in small ventral clumps; leather carp, as their name implies, are generally devoid of scales and display a tough leathery skin, and one variant has a layer of very fine transparent scales over the whole of its body.

Growth rates

Carp are a very fast-growing fish and under ideal conditions in Ireland they may reach 5-10lb (2.5-4.5kg) in four years. They are a very long-lived fish and carp of fifty years of age have been recorded. They continue to grow throughout their life and may reach 80lb (36g). The present Irish record stands at 24lb 14oz (11kg) but the British record is a magnificent 51lb (23kg) mirror carp.

Although they feed well during mild spells in winter, they largely cease to feed when temperatures drop below 8°C. They truly revel in warm water and actively forage and wallow about at temperatures between 20° and 25°C.

Feeding habits
Carp feed extensively on invertebrates and included in their diet are plankton (as juveniles), midge larvae, insect larvae, worms, snails and mussels. They also feed on plant material and are very fond of the seeds of both plants and algae. They frequently 'sieve' through mud and push great clouds of sediment into suspension as they uproot submerged and emergent vegetation. They can penetrate up to 13cm or more when feeding and the accompanying water discoloration frequently inhibits the growth of the softer submerged plants.

Restocking
Carp are ideally suited to a continental-type climate, with very warm but relatively short summers and long cold winters. In Ireland, therefore, they are at the limit of their distribution and, apart from a few exceptional locations, stocks must be periodically maintained by restocking. Carp ova require several weeks of warm summer weather to ripen in the female; with average water temperatures of 14° to 17°C. Spawning takes place at water temperatures of 20°C or above and each female lays between 120 000 and 150 000 ova per kilogram of body weight. Such conditions only occur sporadically in Irish waters. There is also some evidence to suggest that if mature carp fail to spawn for several consecutive seasons they may become wholly or partially sterile. Carp mature at three to four years of age, with the males being the first to mature.

Carp angling

When carp fishing, more than with any other species, time spent in reconnaissance will pay handsome dividends; observe the habits and favourite haunts of the cruising fish; their size and even more importantly their reaction to free offerings of ground bait.

Carp are probably the most intelligent of our freshwater fishes and have an enormous capacity to learn and to remember. On one occasion when we were breeding carp, I began to feed the wild brood fish with bread crust each lunchtime. Within three days these completely wild creatures would actually poke their mouths out of the water to feed on bread held in my fingers. They only backed away when their lips touched my hot fingertips.

Because of the carp's potentially great size and intelligence, an elitist cult of carp anglers has developed in Britain, whose principal goal is to delude monster carp which have previously been caught many times and have learned from that experience. Some such addicts also hold the view that carp of less than 10lb (4.5kg) are not worth catching. This is quite erroneous and I think the true situation was best summed up by Richard Walker, holder for many years of the British record, with a common carp of 40lb (18.1kg), who stated:

> Any carp over 2lb (1kg) is worth catching, one over 10lb (4.5kg) is a big one, one over 15lb (6.5kg) is a monster, and a 20-pounder (9kg) ought to be big enough to satisfy anyone. Anything upwards of 30lb (14kg) is not so much a feat of angling as a matter of biological interest.

Tackle

Carp anglers normally use quite powerful tackle, for they are exceptionally strong fish and may prove difficult to handle in heavily weeded ponds. A standard carp rod would be a 10 to 11ft (3m), through-action, 1½–2½lb (680g–1kg) test curve, carbon fibre or fibreglass rod. Lines vary from 6 to 15lb (2.5–6.5kg) depending on the size of the quarry. An extra large landing net is required for really large carp and specialists often use a 36in (90cm) diameter frame. Proportionately lighter tackle will, of course, suffice in situations where the carp are known to be small.

Bait

Bait and ground bait for carp come under four main headings: bread, naturals, seed/particle bait and specials.

Dried crust is very much a standard bait for carp and may be either legered or free-lined. Flake and paste (see page 151), particularly with a few maggots added, are also favourite baits. More recently, carp anglers have taken to baking their own super-buoyant high-protein bread.

Amongst the so-called naturals are maggots, worms, casters, wasp-grubs, slugs, crayfish, corr-bait and freshwater mussels. These may be fished on standard leger or float rigs; they also make excellent ground bait if used sparingly.

Seed/particle bait has recently grown in popularity, particularly since the development of the 'hair rig' described below. A whole range of baits is used including hemp-seed, sultanas, sweetcorn, various forms of beans and peas, currants, trout pellets and rice.

So-called specials include a range of baits originally pioneered by carp anglers but now used extensively for other coarse fish species. They include luncheon meat, pet foods, cheeses, a selection of human and animal foodstuffs made into paste. Such baits require binders to solidify the mixture; flour or breadcrumbs are often used.

Perhaps the most exciting bait currently in use is the boilie. These high-protein, flavoured baits are roughly the same size and shape as a round hard-boiled sweet. You may now purchase a readily prepared mix from which to manufacture boilies. The ingredients are kneaded into a paste which is rolled into balls of the required diameter, usually ¼–1in (0.5–2.5cm). They are boiled in hot water until they float to the surface. Really hard boilies are left in the water for an extra period of time, depending on the degree of hardness required. Floating boilies — also known as *suzzies* or *popups* — are made by grilling the boilies. Both suzzies and boilies were developed for use with the hair rig.

Float fishing

Irish carp are mostly taken on standard leger or running leger tackle (see page 163). However, float fishing may also prove effective, particularly in very shallow water. The lift bite technique, as described for tench, is ideal (see page 199). Free-lining floating bait for carp is very exciting, and because of their fastidious nature you must be extra careful not to grease the last 2ft (60cm) or so of the line. In heavily fished waters some anglers go to extraordinary lengths to raise the line completely off the water so that only the bait may be seen by the carp. Ingenious methods involving tall beach casters, propped up vertically and with the main line attached to the top of a long, heavy float are often used. The surface bait is attached to a dropper some 2 or 3ft (60–90cm) from the float.

Hair rigs

Probably the most significant recent advance in catching carp has been the development of the hair rig. The original concept was to attach the bait (normally a boilie or seeds) to the 'hair' or piece of extra fine nylon tied to the eye or shank of the hook. The bait was not directly impaled onto the hook and so it looked and behaved like similar pieces of bait added in the ground bait. The carp sucks in the bait and with it the attached hook. The hair is attached to the boilie by boring the bait with a needle-sharp instrument (like a bradawl) and passing the nylon through the hold. The boilie is secured by means of a looped hair knot or a hair bead.

There are a great number of variations on the hair rig theme including strings of boilies or seeds and floating suzzies. Small polystyrene balls have also been used on the hair to make it float. The standard hair rig has a needle-sharp outpointed hook, a wide gape and an upturned eye. They are generally used in sizes 2 to 8.

Bolt rigs

Carp anglers frequently use a bolt rig in conjunction with the hair. This is made from an 8 to 10in (20–25cm) strip of soft, braided Terylene or Dacron line (often dyed dark green) attached to the hair rig at one end and a swivel, bead, Arlesey bomb sequence at the other. The carp sucks in the bait, feels the resistance and bolts, thus hooking itself. The softer dyed line in the trace ensures that the bait sits quite naturally. The Terylene may be replaced by multiple strands of fine nylon which fan out when lying on the bottom.

The above are just some of the carp techniques used in hard-fished waters. However, if the fish are willing to accept a simple rig, stick to it until the fish become less co-operative and a little more choosy.

Bolt rig

APPENDIX 1

Carp Stockings in Ireland 1950–1988

County	Water Stocked	Origin	Date	Observations
Westmeath	Ballinderry	Blackwater Pond	1950	Now absent, transferred out of lake
Westmeath	Ballinderry L.	Germany	1951	Stocked as 2 Y.O. approx. 10oz.
Cavan	L. Gowna	Dalkey Pond	1953	5 adults, average weight 5lb.
*Cork	The Lough, Cork	Kilsheelan/Fish Farm	1954/76/77	Grew to approx. 20lb. 80 fish in original stocking.
Offaly	Pond at Pallas Lake	Kilsheelan	1954	Now absent.
Westmeath	Reynella L.	Ballinderry L.	1956	Lake drained, carp transferred.
Sligo	Ardrea L.	Kilsheelan/Fish Farm	1961	150 fish stocked. Now absent.
Sligo	Ballinascarrow L.	Kilsheelan/Fish Farm	1961	150 fish stocked. Now absent.
Monaghan	Capra Lake	Kilsheelan/Fish Farm	1962	200 fish stocked. Now absent.
Cavan	Green L. Killeshandra	Kilsheelan/Fish Farm	1962	200 fish stocked. Now absent.
Cavan	L. Gowna	Kilsheelan/Fish Farm	1963	70–80, 2+ fish and small adults.
Leitrim	Town Lake, Carrickallen	Kilsheelan/Fish Farm	1964	250 fish stocked. Now absent.
Leitrim	Clooncorick L.	Kilsheelan/Fish Farm	1964	250 fish stocked. Now absent.
Cavan	Killamooney L.	Kilsheelan/Fish Farm	1964	150 fish stocked. Now absent.
Cavan	Drumlon L.	Kilsheelan/Fish Farm	1964	1 fish found in 1969.
Kildare	Grand Canal, Prosperous	Kilsheelan	1964/73	Over 100 fish stocked. Now absent (?)
Mayo	Cloonacurry L.	Kilsheelan/Fish Farm	1965	52 fish stocked. Now absent.
Cavan	Town L., Bailieboro	Kilsheelan/Fish Farm	1965	63 fish stocked. Now absent.
Cavan	Puttiaghan L.	Kilsheelan/Fish Farm	1965	50 fish stocked. Now absent.
Cavan	While Lake Coothill	Kilsheelan/Fish Farm	1965	50 fish stocked. Now absent.
Cavan	Derryvalley L.	Kilsheelan/Fish Farm	1965	50 fish stocked. Now absent.
Mayo	Pond, 10km E of Ballina	England	1974	40 small fish stocked, growth good.
Cork	Riordans Pond, Macroom	Kilsheelan/Fish Farm	1974/77	250 fish stocked.
*Westmeath	Galmoylestown L., Mullingar	Fish Farm/The Lough	1975/76/77	1400+ fish stocked, mainly 0+. Growth good.
Dublin	Dog Pond, Phoenix Park	Fish Farm	1976	Present in 1977.
Westmeath	Doolin L.	Fish Farm	1976	Present. Growth fair.
Cork	Dunbogue L.	Fish Farm	1976	520 fish stocked, all 0+.
Cork	Black Road Pond, Macroom	Fish Farm	1976/77	22 adults in 1976, 94 stocked 1977, all 0+.
Cork.	Dineen's Pond, Coachford	Fish Farm	1976/77	119 fish stocked, mainly 0+.
Tipperary	Kilsheelan Pond	The Lough/Fish Farm	1977/78	30+ adults stocked, spawning confirmed.
Dublin	Herbert Park, Dublin	Fish Farm	1977	Good growth, majority removed, early 80s.
Cork	Pond, Fota Island	Fish Farm	1978	250 fish all 2+. Growth good. Now absent. Pollution.

County	Water Stocked	Origin	Date	Observations
Offaly	Cornaher L.	Fish Farm	1978	13 adults, drainage has affected this lake.
Louth	Taffe's Lake, Duleek	Fish Farm	1978	–
Cork	Nohaval Ponds	–	–	–
Roscommon	Roscommon Ponds	–	Late 70s	–
Galway	Kileen's Ponds near Shannonbridge	–	Late 70s	10 adults stocked. Now absent (?)
Dublin	Zoo Pond, Phoenix Park	Fish Farm	Late 70s	–
Kildare	Derries Pond, Vicarstown	–	1982	–
*Westmeath	Ballinafid Lough, Mullingar	Galmoylestown L.	Early 80s	Adults stocked.
Dublin	Grand Canal, near Dublin	–	Early 80s	Stocking by anglers (unauthorised)
Dublin	Royal Canal, Maynooth	–	Early 80s	Stocking by anglers (unauthorised)
Dublin	Royal Canal, near Dublin	–	Early 80s	Stocking by anglers (unauthorised)
Cork	Banteer Ponds	Fish Farm	1984	100, 0+ fish stocked
Cork	O'Sullivan's Ponds, Watergrass Hill	Fish Farm	1984	80, 0+ fish stocked
Cork	O'Reilly's Pond, Watergrass Hill	Fish Farm	1984	100, 0+ fish stocked
Cork	Doneraile Pond	Fish Farm	1984	200, 0+ fish stocked
Wexford	Knocknesilloge Pond, Blackwater	Fish Farm	1984	100, 0+ fish stocked
Wexford	Ballyvaloo Pond, Blackwater	Fish Farm	1984	100, 0+ fish stocked
Wexford	Johnstown Castle	Fish Farm	1984	150, 0+ fish stocked
Cork	Golden Vale Co-Operative, Charleville	Fish Farm	1984	100, 0+ fish stocked
Clare	Kelly's Pond, O'Callaghan's Mills	Fish Farm	1984	–
Westmeath	Ballinafid Lough, Mullingar	Galmoylestown L.	1988	6 fish. Juveniles and adults.

*** Important angling water**

APPENDIX 2

Useful addresses

Central Fisheries Board
Balnagowan
Mobhi Boreen
Glasnevin
Dublin 9
Tel: (01) 379206

Bord Fáilte/Irish Tourist Board
Baggot Street Bridge
Dublin 2
Tel: (01) 765871

Department of Agriculture for Northern Ireland
Fisheries Division
Hut 5 Castle Grounds
Stormont
Belfast BT4 3TA
Tel: Belfast 63939

Foyle Fisheries Commission
8 Victoria Road
Derry BT47 2AB
Tel: (0504) 42100

Northern Ireland Tourist Board
River House
48 High Street
Belfast BT1 2DS
Tel: Belfast 31221

Shannon Regional Fisheries Board
Thomond Weir
Limerick
Tel: (061) 55171

South Western Regional Fisheries Board
1 Nevilles Terrace
Massey Town
Macroom
Co. Cork
Tel: (026) 41221

Southern Regional Fisheries Board
Anglesea Street
Clonmel
Co. Tipperary
Tel: (052) 23624

Eastern Regional Fisheries Board
Mobhi Boreen
Glasnevin
Dublin 9
Tel: (01) 379206

Northern Regional Fisheries Board
Station Road
Ballyshannon
Co. Donegal
Tel: (072) 51435

North Western Regional Fisheries Board
Abbey Street
Ballina
Co. Mayo
Tel: (096) 22788

Western Regional Fisheries Board
Weir Lodge
Earl's Island
Galway
Tel: (091) 63118/119/110

1. IRELAND'S WATER RESOURCES

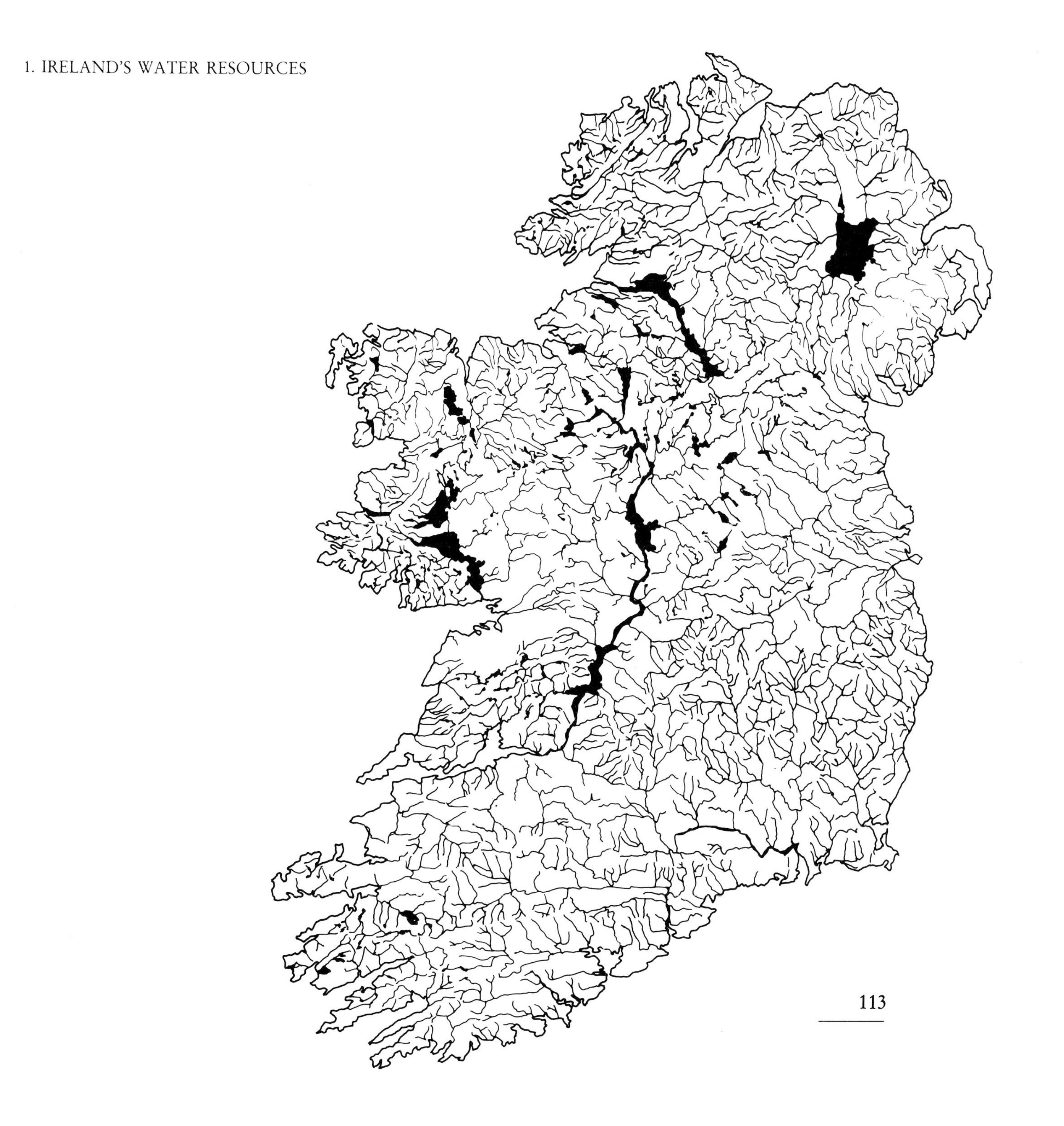

2. COARSE ANGLING CENTRES

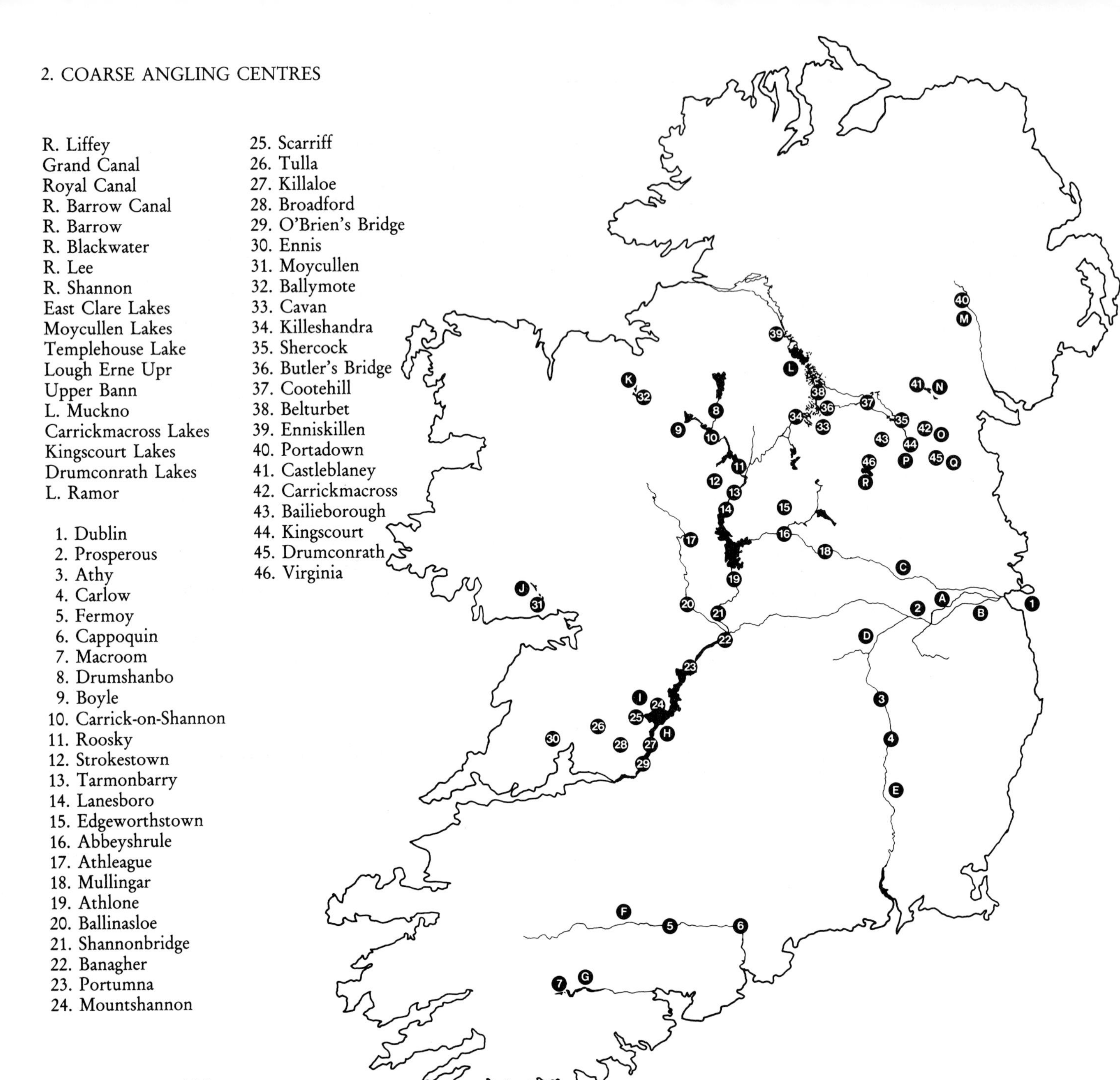

BIBLIOGRAPHY

Angling Guide — Department of Agriculture for Northern Ireland. 108pp

The Angler's Guide — Department of Agriculture, Fisheries Branch, Dublin. (1948) The Stationery Office. 261pp

Annual Reports of the Inland Fisheries Trust. (1951-80) IFT, Glasnevin, Dublin.

BRACKEN, J.J. and CHAMP, W.S.T. (1971) 'Age and growth of pike in five Irish limestone lakes.' Sci. Proc. RDS, Dublin. Ser. B, vol. 3, no.1, 1-33

BULLER, F. (1971) *Pike.* Macdonald and Co. Ltd, London. 1st. edn. 320pp

de BUITLÉAR, ÉAMON (ed.) (1985) *Irish Rivers.* Country House, Dublin. 128pp

FALKUS, H. and BULLER, F. (1988) *Freshwater Fishing.* Stanley Paul, London. 525pp

FITZMAURICE, P. (1981) 'Some aspects of the biology and management of pike (*Esox lucius* L.) stocks in Irish fisheries.' Royal Dublin Society. *J. Life Sci.,* R. Dubl. Soc. 161-173

(1981) 'The spread of roach (*Rutilus rutilus* L.) in Irish waters.' Proc. 2nd. Brit. Fresh. Fish Conf., The University of Liverpool, 13-15 April 1981. 154-161

(1983) 'Carp (*Cyprinus carpio* L.) in Ireland.' *Irish Fish Invest.* Ser. A, no. 23, 5-10

(1984) 'The effects of freshwater fish introductions into Ireland.' EIFAC. Tech. pap. (42) Suppl. vol 2, 449-457

GREAVES, SEAN (1985) (ed.) *The Fishing Handbook.* Beacon Publishing, Northhampton, England.

HAINES, A. and CAMPBELL, M. (1987) *The Angling Times Book of Coarse Fishing.* David & Charles, London. 244pp

HALL, D. (ed.) (1982) *The Match Fisherman.* Pelham Books Ltd, London. 175pp

Irish Sport Fishes — A Guide to their Identification. Central Fisheries Board, Dublin. 66pp

KENNEDY, M. and FITZMAURICE, P. (1968) 'The biology of the bream (*Abramis brama* L.) in Irish waters.' Proc. RIA, vol. 67, sect. B, no. 5. 95-157

KENNEDY, M. (1969) 1. Irish pike investigations. 1. Spawning and early life history. *Irish Fish. Invest.* A, no. 5. 4-33

KENNEDY, M. and FITZMAURICE, P. (1970). 'The biology of the tench (*Tinca tinca* L.) in Irish waters.' Proc. RIA, vol. 69, sect. B, no. 3, 31-82

KENNEDY, M. and FITZMAURICE, P. (1974) 'Biology of the rudd (*Scardinius erythrophthalmus* L.) in Irish waters.' Proc. RIA, vol. 74, sect. B, no.18, 245-303

MORIARTY, C. and HACKETT, N. (1976) 'An exceptionally large eel, *Anguilla anguilla* (L.).' *Ir. Nat. J.* 18, 307-308

MORIARTY, C. (1983) 'Age determination and growth rate of eels, *Anguilla anguilla* (L.).' *J. Fish. Biol.* 23, 257-264

(1986) 'The European eel — discoveries and developments.' Institute of Fisheries Management, 17th Annual Study Course, 9-11 Sept 1986, University of Ulster at Coleraine. 100-110

RICKARDS, B. and WEBB, R. (1971) *Fishing for Big Pike.* Adam and Charles Black Ltd, London. 194pp

RICKARDS, B. (1986) *Angling: Fundamental Principles.* Boydell and Brewer Ltd, Suffolk. 318pp

THORPE, J. (1977) *Synopsis of Biological Data on the Perch — Perca fluviatilis Linnaeus, 1758 and Perca flavescens Mitchill, 1814.* Food and Agriculture Organisation of the United Nations, Rome. FAO Fisheries Synopsis no. 113. 138pp

WALKER, R. (ed.) (1979) *The Shell Book of Angling.* David and Charles Ltd, London. 256pp

WHELAN, K.F. (1981) 'Migratory patterns of bream *Abramis brama* L. shoals in the River Suck system.' *Irish Fish. Invest.* Ser. A, no. 23, 11-15

INDEX